MEET ME AT THE FOUR CORNERS

Stories By

Authors of the

Brampton Writers Guild

Edited by Ken Puddicombe

MiddleRoad | Publishers

"Making Literature see the light of day."

Library and Archives Canada Cataloguing in Publication

Puddicombe, Ken and other authors

Meet Me At The Four Corners

Edited by Ken Puddicombe

ISBN 978-1-7776076-0-9 (soft cover)

Father, Son and Holy Ghost was first published in Commuter Lit October 2020

The One-Legged Tightrope Walker first published Commuter Lit February 2021

Sikander was published in *Perfect Execution And Other Stories* 2017 by MiddleRoad Publishers

The Underground was 2nd Prize winner in Wherever We Roam Collection of Canadian Short Stories

A version of *Best Before* was published in *Down Independence Boulevard And Other Stories* by MiddleRoad Publishers

Man Of The House was condensed in *A Barber's Son* by Eleventh Street Press

A version of *The Man Who Never Was* published in *Down Independence Boulevard And Other Stories* by MiddleRoad Publishers

Front Cover Photo *Four Corners* © courtesy of Ken Puddicombe

Back Cover Photo ©by Herman Brinkman from FreeImages

Cover design by Ken Puddicombe

"Writing is its own reward."

—Henry Miller—

DEDICATED

To all writers who yearn for an outlet for their vivid
imagination

Table of Contents

INTRODUCTION
Michael Joll

The germ of the idea to produce an anthology of the work of the Brampton Writers Guild came early in 2020. It had been at least fifteen years since we had last produced an anthology; time enough for our members to have written some memorable stories.

To encourage entries, as President of the Guild along with Ken Puddicombe, owner and publisher of MiddleRoadPublishers, we decided to start the ball rolling by running a contest for members only. We retained two outside judges to review the entries and in October 2020 we announced the prize winners—three each for fiction and non-fiction. We have included these six winning stories in this volume.

Our members come, if not from the four corners of the earth, at last count from four different continents—North and South America, Europe and Asia. We have taken often circuitous routes to Brampton, but we all have one thing in common: we are proud to call Brampton our home. We meet, when COVID-19 allows us, at the Brampton Library's Four Corners Branch, 65 Queen Street East and we would like to extend our sincere thanks to the Brampton Library and their wonderful, helpful staff for not only providing us with a meeting room but for making us so welcome there.

We are proud of our work which stems from a love of the written word. We hope you will enjoy reading our stories in the aptly titled *MEET ME AT THE FOUR CORNERS* as much as we enjoyed crafting them for you.

Michael Joll,
President, The Brampton Writers' Guild.
February 2021

1. *MY* FOUR CORNERS
By Mark Blair

Queen and Main is Brampton's downtown, an old place suffering from a mid-life crisis. Suddenly, it has taken up a strenuous exercise program of activities: patios, markets, concerts, plays, tambourines and drums; and bedecked itself in new banners, cobblestones, lights, flashing ads and a big screen. It is an intersection desperately trying to distance itself from its frumpy past. A corner east, as a maiden might bow, so Queen Street gracefully undergoes the rail overpass while having on her hips a big brown box of books to grow by. That big brown box is my *Four Corners*.

Its entrance looks as if one corner were knocked in by a boot and painted green. As you walk through its doors, there before you, standing at attention, are its three magical guards right through whom you must walk. And if a book had taken a strong liking and attached itself to you and you were to walk through a guard on leaving, the guard would beep—just three times though. Then from behind her desk some way back, the kindly librarian would smile at you and say, "You must have forgotten to check out an item."

Behind her are many shelves of all kinds of books: short ones, tall ones, fine ones, fat ones, and even the floppy kind. I once asked a total stranger whether he had ever thought to read every single one of them to which his incredulity was apparent even before he had opened his mouth to answer.

"Jus wuh fancies yuh," he said.

He looked Irish. Ales are their thing, so I kept my peace.

At the back of the floor is the Department of Lilliput where small minds play and not care at all that though speech might be silver, silence is positively golden. For them, reading is the exuberance of half-baked vocalizations.

"Jack and Jill went up the hill," one began rather loudly last Tuesday then, slowly turning the page, looked quizzically at the picture on the other side. Beside him, Gulliver stressed, "to fetch…a pail…of whuuh-tuuhr," whereupon the little lad looked up. "Water?" he asked. Meanwhile, a girl of about seven and three quarters was urging her father to find *Tangled*. So, he stood there staring intently at the shelf, walking this way and that, stroking his chin until a friendly librarian came and offered to help.

On the left-hand side of the main aisle are the sofas and, towards the front, rows of moving pictures. Also on that side is the *Insatiable Mouth of Returns*. Put a book on its tongue and in less than a blink, it swallows it whole. It is much the same at the checkout stations further up front, though they do not take your books. They just make mental notes of everything you show them and print the notes out very nicely for you on a long slip of paper. They can be absent-minded though, so you must be careful. Once I borrowed fifteen items and asked for a receipt to which one merely ignored my request as if I had not asked at all and wanted to know if I cared to checkout—as if I had not done so already.

There's a room on the left into which I've never been and an elevator on the right which I've never taken. I use the stairs all the time. I like it because it is the only part of the building which has defied a facelift. Its wide steps, sharp turns and echoes give it an air of medieval times when people lived in castles and dragons roamed wild in the imagination of men. Sometimes, a battalion of teens seems to be coming through, shoes and voices reverberating against the walls; but then it turns out being just two girls from whom you learn, by the way, that "Julie is an effing bitch!" You know, of course, that means war.

Upstairs is the place to be for research and study—and, for the very hungry, a place to munch on chocolate bars too, though the practice is highly frowned upon. The magazine section is particularly conducive to quiet reflection. There, with National Geographic open in front of me, I would often drift off in a daydream, gazing through the wide-open glass walls at the hustle and bustle in the street below or at the concrete garden on the other side. In Brampton, no one likes a naked earth, so trees and plants and delicate flowers are caught between a rock and a hard place.

Beside the stairway as you turn towards the right on reaching the second floor, there is a brown nondescript door, hidden away in a corner bearing the label in plain Arial font: BORED ROOM. It's a misnomer for sure, for all kinds of stories get told within its hallowed walls: conspiracies, murders, mayhem, love, kisses, betrayals, politics, death, sorrow, pain, war, travelogues, high adventure, reflections and the funny tales of pleasant memories.

Within those *Four Corners*, in an executive chair at an executive table, I too get to be me and share my thoughts with those who reflect my passion: for life, for writing, and for marking up the works of others.

And I like it very much.

2. A CUP OF CHAI
By Cherry Narula

Chai, Hindi word for tea, has been crucial for connecting people for centuries and it comes as no surprise that this unifying brew has helped tea drinkers cope during lockdowns.

In our latest Covid Pandemic, people have continued to connect over tea, even though it is being done over Zoom or Google Meet. Tea traditions to connect with friends and family, were only waiting to be tweaked with the help of these innovative ideas and technology. Two friends in Scotland even made it in the news by sharing tea when they brought their folding chairs and flasks of tea to the border between their two councils. They set themselves up four meters apart beneath their council boundary signs. This news about two dear friends enjoying tea together, yet following strict council rules, brought smiles to many faces.

A simple cup of tea has a universal appeal to soothe and calm. After water, tea is the second most popular drink worldwide. Anyone who has travelled on trains in India, can never forget the cheerful calls for *Chai* at railway stations by the *Chaiwallas* (tea vendors). The bliss of drinking that hot, spiced tea in red clay cups with an earthy hue, lingers for years. At the peak of a hot Indian summer, it is popular to hear, "Have a cup of tea, it will cool you." In winter months, the same magical brew "will warm you." This amazing brew is recommended for almost every situation. Versatile to the hilt, it can be sweet, salty, sour, spicy or a blend of various tones. Thus, in a country of more than 1.3 billion, *Chai* is not simply a drink of tea, it is an integral part of life.

The United Nations has recognised that tea has medicinal properties and is beneficial for health.

Many have their memories of tea as a concoction of various spices and herbs used as a remedy for a sore throat. This is an Indian Ayurvedic concoction, traditionally called *Kaadha*, that is popularly used to soothe a cough or cold. Also known as mom's or grandma's special formula, *Kaadha* is recommended for throat infections, as well building immunity. Kaadha, sweetened with honey or jaggery has soothed many a kid during a cold or fever. Commonly, Kaadha is made from spices such as: ginger, fennel, star anise, turmeric, giloy, mint, liquorice, cloves, black pepper, basil, carom seeds, cardamom, and cinnamon boiled together. Some add salt in addition to a sweetener such as honey or jaggery. This can be consumed either with or without milk or lemon. The recipe is flexible to adapt to different climates, seasons and availability of ingredients. This Kaadha is a versatile herbal immunity concoction that has been embraced by many as a part of their daily lifestyle.

India is the second largest exporter of tea in the world and consumes over 70% of the tea it produces. Tea stalls can be found in all cities on almost every street. From the hidden nooks of Himalayan villages to the off-beaten path in the salt desert, tea stalls are everywhere. The Chaiwallas and tea stalls play a vital role in the rhythm of daily life that transcends boundaries. Friendly chit chat, gossip or intense political discussions take place over this small cup of chai, even among strangers. Moreover, India is also home to more than 14,000 tea estates. Many of these are of historical significance and are great places to visit for nature lovers. One such plantation, the Kolukkumalai tea estate, is situated at a height of 7,900 ft above sea level. This tea estate has a small tea factory where leaves are still hand-picked and hand-packaged for distribution.

The innumerable varieties of tea have a flavour to suit each palate: Kangra Tea with hints of earthiness, the fragrant Darjeeling Tea, the mellow Assam Chai, the popular Masala Chai, Mumbai's Cutting Chai, the roasted aroma of Lopchu Tea, floral tones of Nilgiri Tea and so on. The Himalayan white tea from Darjeeling and the second flush Darjeeling Oolong.

Camellia Sinensis and Camellia Assamica are exclusive varieties. Apart from these, there is the unique preparation of butter tea and the Kashmiri Pink Chai also known as Gulabi Chai, Noon Chai or Shir Chai. Butter tea is ideal for high altitude Himalayan regions. Thick, buttery tea is made by soaking crushed brick tea overnight in water, followed by churning it with salt, goat's milk, and yak butter. Kashmiri Chai is perfect for cold weather and is topped with crushed nuts, infused with spices, salt and baking soda as key ingredients. Baking soda gives it the rosy hue and salt prevents dehydration at high altitudes.

The first International Tea Day was celebrated in New Delhi in 2005. Sri Lanka also started observing it in 2006 and more countries followed to celebrate December 15 as International Tea Day. In 2015, India proposed a global recognition of 'International Tea Day' to the United Nations Food and Agriculture Organisation. This led to the International Day of Tea being celebrated worldwide on May 21 chosen to coincide with the season of tea production in most tea producing countries. The International Tea Day is significant for public events, seminars and celebration of tea culture. Challenges faced by tea plantations and its workers are discussed, remedies are presented and steps to implement changes are approved. This day is also popular for creative tea recipe posts on social media, accompanied by amusing and nostalgic tea related memories.

The different types of tea enjoyed in various ways also highlight cultural diversity worldwide. In the east, in China, green tea is vital for health benefits, hospitality traditions and ancestral ceremonies. In Japan, the *Tea Ceremony* is historic and an important part of Japanese culture. The tea ceremony includes the tradition of how it is prepared as well as the manner in which it is consumed. This ceremony is representative of harmony, tranquility, purity and respect. In Taiwan, the popular Pearl Milk Tea with tapioca balls comes in various innovative varieties. These can be in the form of fruity iced tea or milk tea similar to a milkshake. This bubble tea has become very popular with the younger generation all over the world.

In Britain, *High Tea* and *Afternoon Tea* have been a tradition with popular black tea blends like English Breakfast and Earl Grey. It comes as no surprise that Britain has some of the most delightful tea rooms in the world. Even a city like Paris, well known for its café culture, has a history of remarkable Salons de Thé'. The oldest, Mariage Freres, first opened its tearoom in 1854. Experts are present in the salon to help choose the perfect tea. An ancient tea museum can be visited on the first floor. Another renowned Salon de Thé, Carette, opened in Place du Trocadéro in 1927.

In North America, protests over high taxes on imported tea in 1773, led to the well-known history of the Boston Tea Party. Three shiploads of tea were dumped into the harbour by protestors.

Tea has been consumed as both a hot and cold beverage in the United States and Iced tea gained widespread popularity as a thirst-quenching drink a century ago. Since then, innovative iced tea recipes made their way into recipe books and menus and now, tea plantations can be found in the United States primarily in Alabama, California, Georgia, Florida and Hawaii. Canada's only tea farm is located in British Columbia where Westholme Tea Company in the Cowichan Valley has a tea shop, gallery of imported teas and an 11-acre organic tea farm.

Thousands of years of the history of tea spans across the world along with a treasure trove of stories. These are accompanied by an inheritance of traditions bringing friends and family together. In any single get-together, it is not uncommon to find everyone relishing a distinct brew. The flavours and aromas of tea continue to evolve tremendously to include infusions of diverse roots, flower petals and herbs.

A stress buster for many, the unique charm of each blend brings nature into our lives with each new cup of chai.

3. THE MAN WHO NEVER WAS
By Ken Puddicombe

He had an uncontrollable itch on his scalp, working its way down the right side of his face, culminating in the area of his neck. And pain—excruciating, searing and piercing pain like he'd never experienced.

He badly wanted to reach the source of his discomfort and when he tried he could feel the upper muscles of his right arm tightening, and yet, he was unable to move it up to his head. Had he been amputated at the elbow?

Sounds. All around: the shuffle of feet, the rustle of clothing, and murmuring—a sigh, a moan, a groan. He detected them all, because these were the only sounds he heard in the otherwise deathlike silence.

And darkness, too. Darkness was familiar to him, though. He recalled being in the dark with other people. He couldn't see them, but he knew they were there from what he heard, and he also knew they were all in the same predicament. But what *was* the predicament? Was it all a dream?

He wondered if he was still alive. Or was he trapped somewhere in the afterlife? If so, how did he get there? He couldn't remember.

He raised his head, looked down and realized his right hand was strapped to the side of a bed, but his left hand was free. He moved it towards his head. He wanted to satisfy his craving, but he was stopped short by a shout.

"Don't," the voice said. It was female, strong and powerful and coming out of a void. It had a sense of urgency too, and a tone that spelled authority. Was he now in heaven? Was God female, after all?

The voice continued. "If you scratch at it the area will get infected and only make things a lot worse. And we don't want that, do we?"

Of course he didn't want that. But why was he subject to infection in the first place?

He traced the bandage wrapped over his head, down the right side of his face and around his neck. He was unable to see clearly—his right eye was covered. The woman was there in the room, though. She came out of the shadows of the dimly lit aisle and he deciphered the blurred outline of a white uniform.

He said, "Who…you?" His voice came out as a squeak.

"Welcome back, Mister Singh," she said.

Singh? Why was she calling him *Singh*? His name was Persaud. Why they change his name?

"You had us worried for a while, Ram Singh," the voice continued.

Singh. There was something familiar about the name. Had he been reincarnated in someone else's body? He rifled his brain to find the answer, but it kept eluding him.

"Who you be?" he demanded.

"You don't remember me? I'm disappointed. And with all the time I've been spending with you. Nurse Hackett."

"Is where I am, nurse?"

"You're in the burn ward at Bellevue Hospital."

Burns…burns…burns…he was on the way to work in the mailroom. That much he recalled. There was a fire, or a bomb exploded, or something like that. It was coming back to him. Of course, Singh was his new name, the one he'd adopted after coming to America.

"How long I been here?"

"Tuesday afternoon. We've had you on sedatives and antibiotics."

"What day is today?"

"It's Friday."

He looked around. He made out the silhouette of beds, occupied by people looking like Egyptian mummies and enclosed in a plastic bubble, an oxygen tank at the bedside.

"How bad I get burn?"

She came and stood over him as she checked his pulse. She was even larger than he had thought. Her hand encircled his; hers a shade of ebony contrasting even with his brown tone. When she smiled, she did so with her entire face: cheeks, forehead, eyes and all.

"You suffered first and second degree burns," she said.

"Will I be okay?"

"Do you mean are you going to live? The answer is yes. You were lucky. Many didn't make it. The right side of your body received the worst of it, from your head to your neck. Your right eye was also badly scalded."

"I seem to remember something about a bomb exploding in the tower, or something like that."

"It was a jet. Not one, two jets. Both towers."

Something stirred in his memory. "I believe I used to work in the mail room, on the one hundred and first floor. How long more will I be here?"

"The whole complex was destroyed. You're going to be transferred to the recovery area tomorrow. I think they will send you home in a few days. We've been giving you cold baths since you were brought in. Your neck and upper torso were also burnt." She looked at the area below his waist. "Below that, everything seems to be in good working order. I could tell when I was sponging you."

A man approached her, pulling a trolley with hospital gowns and porter uniforms. "Where do you want this delivery?"

"Just put them in the cupboard and take the soiled ones," she told him. She turned away and headed for the nurse's station.

Ram watched as the man went to the cupboard. He was wearing overalls, blue, long sleeves, pockets top and bottom, just like the ones Ram wore when he sorted mail…

*

The day had started out like any other.

He was expecting another hectic eight hours and heading up to the 110th floor. Processing the daily mail for over four hundred companies with twenty thousand employees was not an easy task, not even after his years of experience in various positions. It had been a long, hard climb, starting with making deliveries, moving up to sorter, rising to the supervisor's position.

The trip up to the mailroom required a change in elevators after riding the express up to the 78th floor. He was waiting for the local with five other people—two women and three men.

He was watching the floors count down from the 110th, when he felt the building shudder. It seemed to sway, move forward, backwards and forward again, like a drunken sailor after a night of indulgence. They all fell to the floor.

"What the hell in God's name just happened?" one of the men said. His brown-haired toupee lay lop-sided on his head.

"I don't believe this," the second man said. He looked at his watch. "I'm going to be late for my meeting."

Ram Singh looked at *his* watch: it was 8:47. Mail delivery was going to be late—the first time since his promotion.

The lights flickered, went out and cloaked the floor in darkness. He heard noises coming from the offices. One of the women in his group screamed, the other squawked. The one who screamed was closer to him and it was deafening, but nothing close to the rumble filling his ears from the upper floors. It sounded as if the *A Train* he took every morning to work had been rerouted through the top floors of the Tower.

The emergency lights kicked in.

He got off the floor. His legs were rubbery; he felt as if he'd missed a mail sack thrown from the driver of the delivery truck and been hit over the head.

A large group, about twenty-five or thirty men and women rushed out of the offices.

"It's best not to take the elevator at a time like this," a man from the Thai Farmers Bank said. He was short, bald, and dressed in a light blue business suit. He looked like someone accustomed to taking control of a situation. He headed for *Stairway A*, one of three emergency exits, and everyone followed him.

A debate started: Should they go up or down?

"I think it was a bomb," the banker said. "I could feel it all the way down to the foundation. Remember the blast in New York? Best to go to the top floor and wait for rescue." He headed up the stairs and half of the group followed him.

A man in a grey suit had been on his cell phone from the moment he came out of the offices. He said, "It wasn't a bomb. It was a plane. A frigging jet plane crashed into one of the top floors." His voice grew angry. "Was the pilot blind or what?"

"Might have been mechanical failure," a woman volunteered.

"Don't know about the rest of you," Grey Suit said, "but I'm heading *down* to the ground floor. If we head up, we can easily get cut off if this damn thing expands to more floors."

Seventy-eight floors—two flights of stairs for every floor. Ram had counted them once, when the elevators were out of commission due to a power outage.

He found himself shuffling down the stairwell. He knew he would make it to ground floor. Hadn't they said, so many times, that the building was safe and impenetrable, able to withstand anything thrown at it?

There were hundreds of others making their way down, and soon, it started to feel like rush hour on the subway, only it was orderly, as if people didn't believe there was urgency in the exodus.

Three flights down, acrid smoke started to fill the stairwell. He heard creaking, groaning, moaning in the walls, and he deciphered the messages: *Hurry. Hurry. There's not much time left.*

Shortly after the 60th floor, he heard a second explosion, a muffled sound that had little impact on the North Tower, but it was close.

"Another jet plane crashed into the South Tower," Grey Suit with the cell phone said.

"No frigging way that's an accident," a man said. "It's terrorists."

It was at this time that people started to pick up the pace.

On the 58th floor: temperature rising; stifling heat, almost impossible to touch the rails going down.

On the tenth floor: It started to rain, water spiralling through the ceilings and walls and soon they were wading. Men sloshed around in soggy pants and women kicked off shoes. Grey Suit pulled his jacket over his head and Ram heard snatches: "Don't know…what's waiting for us…Love you too honey…tell kids I love them…"

The older woman in front of him missed a step. Then, her heel snagged on the metal edge of a riser and she was down in an instant, inert like a sack after it was dumped from the U.S. mail truck. In a flash people piled up on top of her.

Ram said, "Yuh okay lady? Want some help?" he asked, but she looked at him blankly, as if he'd addressed her in a foreign tongue.

Grey Suit put away his cell phone. "Do you need some help?"

She looked at her right foot. "I think I sprained my ankle."

"Wanna give me a hand to take her down?" Grey Suit said to Ram.

Water now came down in cataracts, through the walls and from the stairwell above. Together, Ram and Grey Suit started to portage the injured woman down the stairwell.

Finally, they reached the lobby with their load.

Ram had walked through the lobby thousands of times and knew it inside out, but now, it defied recognition. The massive chandeliers lay in shattered heaps, the crystals and bulbs lying like cheap glass on the floor. The marbled walls had collapsed and were stacked in staggered Pompeian mounds. The revolving doors had blown outwards, leaving their bare metal frames standing as silent sentinels to a bygone era where they controlled the flow of people. The floor had become a wading pool and the elevator doors had blown outwards and were lying on the floor like sheet metal waiting for rehabilitation.

He'd never seen such devastation. He imagined what it would be like after a nuclear bomb exploded.

Ambulance attendants were waiting and two of them took over the transportation of the woman.

"I'm going back up to see if anyone else needs help," Grey Suit said. In another minute he had disappeared up the stairwell.

Ram was standing by the elevator, pondering whether he had the stamina to return to the stairwell, when he heard a swoosh from above. Instinct kicked in; he moved away from the shaft. Just then, the swoosh turned to a splat as something struck the top of the elevator car. He turned his head to avoid the impact of the liquid fireball, but he wasn't quick enough.

Had it really taken the eternity it felt like to get to the ambulance? His lasting images were those of a cascade of debris falling from above as the building relinquished ownership of its contents. Furniture—chairs, desks, drawers that once stored secrets and unseen contents would now make the light of day. Paper—reams of it fluttering and sailing on wind-streams. Were they letters he'd delivered? The bombardment blocked the sun but he was sure he saw bodies plummeting in free-fall.

*

Nurse Hackett said, "Today's a big day for you."

"Why?" he mumbled.

"The mayor and city councillors will be coming tomorrow morning, along with radio, newspaper and television crews."

"Why they coming?"

"To see you. You're a celebrity."

"Don' feel like one."

"Not to mention, you're a hero. There's talk of a medal."

He squirmed. "Don' really want that."

"The whole country wants to hear your story."

She did a one hundred and eighty scan of the ward. No one was within hearing distance. "Don't think you know," she whispered, "but there's a big payout for all the victims. Money is coming from all directions—Federal, State, City, plus insurance. You might be looking at a cool million dollars in your pocket. And free medical treatment for the rest of your life."

It was a staggering sum, something that would take him several lifetimes to earn. He thought of all he could do with it—clear his mortgage, pay off his debts, take a vacation, and still have a tidy sum left over for retirement.

Then, there was the outstanding amount for his Green Card. He still owed ten thousand dollars, including interest, for which he was making monthly instalments. His contact who knew a contact who knew a contact in the Immigration and Naturalization Service would be happy to receive the entire amount.

But, he realized, with consternation, the reward would bring scrutiny from the media. They'd be taking pictures, probing into his background, making a big deal of what he'd done. His picture would be plastered over every newspaper and someone who knew him from way back was sure to recognise him. Eventually they would find out he'd been on the run.

It had been a stroke of luck when he made contact through a friend who'd gone the same route. At first, he'd hesitated. Being able to purchase residency and a green card? It sounded too good to be true. Nothing was negotiated directly with the person in the department. That was the way they did things. It was always someone who knew someone who knew someone.

The Green Card and Social Insurance for his new identity were real. He knew that, realized it every time he'd presented it to all the employers he'd worked for. But somewhere, in some cemetery, there was a man by the name of Ram Singh, long since dead and buried. As common as the name might be, someone was bound to add two and two. What if the contact in the Immigration Service was caught one day? Discovery would mean being deported to Guyana, him and his entire family, without the money.

In Guyana, yet another wave of publicity would follow. His ex-wife Julie would find out he was alive and living under a different identity in America.

He settled back into the bed. "How many more like us?"

Nurse Hackett sighed. "No one knows for sure right now. Might be thousands dead, a lot more injured. It will take weeks before the final count comes in."

"Do they know who did it?"

"Al Keeda's taken responsibility, along with Bin Lading. President Bush is promising to make them pay."

In the North Tower, there were about twenty-five thousand visitors and workers on an average day. He wondered how many of those had survived.

*

It was dark, apart for a nightlight in the nurse's station. Ram had seen Nurse Hackett go on her break.

He eased out of bed, the pain surging through his right side. He headed for the staff locker. It was open. The porter's civilian clothes were there. He took off his gown and tugged the shirt over his shoulder, pulled up the pants and slipped on the pair of shoes which were too large but would do for now.

They'd be looking for him, come morning.

Ram Singh would be long gone by then and he was nevvah coming back.

4. REUNITED

[3rd PRIZE FICTION BWG 2020 COMPETITION]

By Lynda Brunelle

"Sawyer!" Candace Walker screamed at the top of her lungs, her heart pounding in her chest. "Sawyer! Where are you?"

She ran through the woods, feeling more frantic, screaming his name. Every once in a while, she'd stop and listen for him but all she could hear was the wind rustling through the leaves. Her dog had never run away like this. She looked up at the sky which was getting darker and the smell of distant rain filled her nostrils. The knot in her stomach grew tighter. Where was he?

A low rumble of thunder in the distance had her scream Sawyer's name again. She didn't want to wander too far from where he'd ran off. He loved chasing squirrels, but he always came back. In her search, she 'd wandered into a part of the woods she wasn't familiar with, but she had to find her dog. Sawyer was everything to her. Why did she let him off the leash?

She thought she heard a bark. She yelled his name again. Please let that be him and please let him come back. She needed him safe and sound. A fat tear rolled down her cheek and she swiped it away quickly. She couldn't cry. She had to find him and keep her emotions in check. Once his furry body was in her arms, she could cry all she wanted.

The wind picked up and Candace glanced up at the sky, hoping by some miracle it would be blue. Unfortunately, it was turning ominously dark. Why hadn't she checked the weather before she went out?

She heard the bark again and this time it sounded closer. She rushed towards the sound, swiping at branches as she ran. Out of the corner of her eye she saw a wagging white tail and an overwhelming sense of relief rushed over her. She called his name and Sawyer came running to her. Candace swept him up in her arms, burying her face in his warm, soft neck and sobbing with relief.

"This your dog?"

Candace looked up, startled to see a man standing in front of her. A man she knew. She was overwhelmed with emotion. Gordon McFarland. Twenty years older but still handsome as the devil. Last time she'd seen him was the night she told him the wedding was off.

His lips parted. "Candace? Is that you?"

She stood up and gave him a rueful smile, aware her face must be covered in tear-stained mascara and she looked a mess. "Gordon. Wow. This is a surprise."

Thunder cracked over them, causing her to jump. Sawyer whimpered.

Gordon held out his hand. "Come with me. We need to get out of this storm. Now."

She didn't hesitate. His callused hand felt large and safe and familiar in hers. The rain came down fast and heavy as he led them to safety.

Safety was a log cabin deep in the woods. Gordon held the door open for her and Sawyer and they entered. The door slammed shut behind them, carried by a gust of wind. Sawyer shook his wet body, sending droplets flying, and he raced around the living area, trying to get dry. He jumped on the couch, finding a wool blanket, and rolled his body around it.

Candace gave Gordon an apologetic smile. "Sorry about him."

Gordon was looking at her with a picture of shock and surprise. He ran his hand through his dark, wet hair and shook his head. "Candace Walker. You have a dog."

"I do," Candace gave him an apologetic grin. "Can you believe it?"

"No," Gordon shook his head. "If I didn't see it with my own eyes. You were a diehard cat person. What happened to Hunter?"

A sad look crossed Candace's face. "He passed away. He had a long and good life, though. I had a friend who adopted Sawyer as a puppy, but she broke her back and could no longer care for him. I took him and he's been the best thing to happen to me."

"Dogs are something else. I'm glad you finally came to the dog side. There's no going back after."

A flash of lightning lit up the cabin and the lights flickered. Gordon jumped into action, grabbing a flashlight from the table and lighting some candles.

"I'll make a fire," he said, as the lights flickered again and finally going out for good. Within moments he had a roaring fire going. Candace shivered again and moved closer to the fire to warm up.

"Let me get you some dry clothes. You're soaked."

He disappeared and a moment later he returned with a pair of grey joggers and a hoodie which Candace accepted gratefully. She quickly changed into the oversized and cozy clothes. They smelled freshly laundered and Candace inhaled the scent, relishing it. Nothing felt as good as changing out of wet clothes and into oversized men's clothes.

"Beer?" Gordon offered her as she sat back down in front of the fire on the floor. "Sorry, it's all I have and with no power I can't make you a coffee."

"That's fine, I'll take the beer."

They sat in an uncomfortable silence for a few moments, the only sounds being the rain pounding on the door, the cackling fire and Sawyer softly snoring from the couch. Candace kept stealing glances at Gordon. He had changed little over the years. His eyes had some crinkles around them when he smiled and white streaks peppered his beard, but other than that he seemed the same man to whom she was once engaged. Her heart lurched, thinking of the last time she'd seen him. The hurt in his face when she handed him back his ring had haunted her. She always wondered if she'd made the right decision.

"Why are you here?" He said, never one to beat around the bush.

"I lost my dog and then a storm came," she smiled, attempting to make a joke, but he didn't smile back. She sighed. "I'm living with my father. He had a fall and is having trouble with his mobility. And I lost my job."

He raised his eyebrows but said nothing.

She took a sip of her beer, then snuck another glance at him. "How are you? What have you been up to?"

He motioned around him. "This."

She furrowed her brows. "What's this?"

"This. Living here."

"How are you making a living? Is this a homestead?"

He threw his head back and laughed. "No, it 's not a homestead. I am on the grid. I have internet and other modern-day comforts. Come and I'll show you why I 'm living here." He held out his hand to her and she accepted, feeling a rush as his big hand enveloped hers and he helped her up from the floor.

He led her up a set of stairs and Candace gasped. The view from the floor to ceiling windows was incredible. Even through the pouring rain, she could see the snow-capped mountains in the distance. She looked at him in awe.

"I had no idea you could get this view so close to town."

A crack of thunder—so loud it made Candace jump—sounded like it was directly overhead. The wind howled and what looked like a tree branch came slamming against the window. Gordon grabbed her hand and they went back downstairs where Sawyer was still sleeping, oblivious of the active weather outside.

"Do you need to call your dad? Or your husband?"

Candace shook her head. "Husband? I don 't have a husband. But I do need to get in touch with my father."

She quickly phoned her father, who reassured her he was fine. When she disconnected the call, she could feel Gordon staring at her. His steel-blue eyes looking and searching. She opened her mouth to say something, but nothing came out. There was so much to say, yet nothing to say.

"Was it worth it?" Gordon said, breaking the silence between them. The wind howled outside, and something banged against the side of the house, but he seemed unfazed.

"Was what worth it?" She was being deliberately obtuse. She didn't want to face him, with everything in her life hurling towards this moment.

"Leaving. Calling our wedding off. Was it worth it? Did you lead the life you dreamed of? The life that didn't include me?"

Tears threatened to betray her, and she blinked rapidly to make them stop, turning away from him. "I never meant to hurt you."

He sighed loudly and sat down on the couch next to Sawyer, his hand reaching out to stroke the dog's soft fur. Candace felt her heart melt watching him be so gentle and loving to her pup.

"I know that Candace. It took me a while to get over it, but I did. Seeing you now just stirred up some things. You look as beautiful as you did when you were twenty."

Candace sat down on the couch, on the other side of Sawyer. Instinctively, her hand reached out to pet her puppy and she and Gordon's hands touched. A jolt of electricity flew through her as she quickly withdrew her hand. She glanced at him. He was the one that got away, even though their breakup was all her doing. In the twenty years since she'd last seen him, he was still the best man she'd ever been with. He was kind and rugged and handsome. He appeared in her dreams periodically, and it was still a shock to see him here in the flesh.

"I was let go," Candace blurted. "The newspaper restructured, and I found myself out of a job."

"I'm sorry to hear that," Gordon said, his voice full of empathy.

Candace shrugged. "It's the way of the world now. I couldn't afford to live in the city without my salary, so I came home with my tail between my legs. And here we are. So yes, I regret leaving you. If I'd have stayed, we would have had three kids and a beautiful life here in the mountains and two dogs."

"You wanted none of that," Gordon said, his voice gentle. "You wanted a fast city life. You wanted excitement and travel and you wanted nothing to do with my boring life."

She blinked, feeling a rush of remorse at her younger self. She crossed her arms over her chest. "You're right. I did, and I got it."

"And now you're back where you started. With me."

Her heart skipped a beat. "Yes."

A clap of thunder sounded overhead, but Candace didn't flinch. She felt safe and warm sitting in front of a roaring fire with her pup next to her and the man she once loved. For the first time in a long time, she felt safe. Like she was finally home.

5. COMPOSITIONS ANONYMOUS

[1st PRIZE FICTION BWG 2020 COMPETITION]

By Mark Blair

For many months now, I've been suffering from a writer's block. It was my fault really. At a book launch, I thoroughly disagreed with the author. Afterwards, she took vengeance and banged me in the head with her book. WHAM! And I immediately fainted. When I recovered, I was in bed and the nurse in the ward, having stuck her thermometer in my mouth but seeing that I had come to my senses, frantically pulled it out.

"You're HOT!" she cried, looking curiously at it.

"What do you mean by that?" I demanded.

"FORTY degrees!" she said.

I was in an oven for sure, drenched in perspiration. I tried to get up but she placed her palm on my chest, and I sank back into the damp sheets.

"Ok," I said weakly. "This time you win."

The door swung open and in rushed another, madly wheeling a wheelchair. She deftly steered it to my side and the two of them lifted me bodily into it, huffing and puffing. And me? I was feeling deliciously light the whole time. Then off we went to the elevator, up to the tenth floor which, when the door parted, presented a spectacle of wide, open-concept space. The high ceiling and windows reduced my presence to ridiculous insignificance. Even the furniture looked like lost lambs huddling in little flocks. In the distant corner, a gaggle of old folk in white were arguing over something or other, the lively tiff becoming clearer the nearer we got to their circle of chairs, until I was put among them. They fell silent.

"This is Mark," the voice over my head announced. "Be kind and welcome him."

"Hi Mark," the chorus of voices replied. "Welcome to our chapter."

"Thank you."

"What is your part of speech, Mark?"

I drew a blank and in the ensuing silence, bore the brunt of their collective stares.

"What, what?" I stammered. "What do you mean?"

"Your part of speech," they urged in chorus again.

"Noun?"

At this, everyone burst into loud applause.

"Nouns are good," one said, and they all started echoing each other, nodding approvingly. "Nouns are good."

An elderly man, slightly bent, shakily stepped to the podium. He cleared his throat. The microphone screeched. He waited, then raised a shaky hand and pointed a bony finger at each person, counting those present. After shakily writing the number down, he began mumbling into the microphone. Everyone sat respectfully silent and dutifully attentive until he had finished and shakily returned to his seat.

Thereafter a more youthful one sprang forward, a woman in flats. She strode flat-footed to the podium and tapped twice on the microphone.

"Goood evenin', youw people," she began folksily, her voice booming across the entire floor. "I see we aou all pwesent today plus wan. Welcome again, Mauhwk. We've huhwd so much about you, as I'm shua, you of us too."

What? I never heard of these people.

"My name is Ono Matapoeia, as ehvweone knows; and today we'uhw adding twee bwand new wouhds to English. Isn't dat won-duhw-ful?"

More like a hundred, I thought; but was overpowered by the standing ovation at her announcement.

"We aou pwivileged to have wid us, Miss Mesmowize who has witten a book abowt duh … 'ole … ting."

She paused. "Miss Mesmowize …"

Everyone turned to look at Miss Mesmowize who had gotten up and gone wandering away from the group, calling out urgently to a phantom. The nurses ran, calmed and patiently brought her back to the podium where in a sudden turn of presence, she demonstrated remarkable command of herself, the group and language. One of the nurses came over and lifted my chin since my mouth had fallen open in astonishment.

"Thank you, Fraulein Chairman," she began with extemporaneous eloquence. "Pursuant to Article One, spelt, ONE, one, of our mandate, I was engaged in first determining the extent of common parlance of the wordoids which Ono Matapoeia suggested three months and one score days ago, and secondly, finding that their use was non-existent, in preparing a case for their adoption in English which you can read about in greater detail than I plan on delving into this evening, in my new book, *Words That Could Do Something: A Serious Case For Wham, Bang, and Poof.* Given the gravity of their potential, I have divided my talk into two paragraphs."

I couldn't believe my ears.

"I propose," she continued, "that the meanings applied to the trio of NEW terms be similar yet distinctively progressive, starting with *wham* and ending with *poof* on a linguistic continuum. In summary, hereafter, may it be established that to *wham* is to strike something forcefully, to *bang*...well, you get the idea, and *poof* be used to convey the suddenness with which someone or something disappears." She paused to lick her lips then drily said, "This is the end of my talk. Any questions? Comments..."

I just couldn't take it anymore than you, dear reader. My hand shot up.

"Those three words are old," I protested.

Everyone sat stone-faced.

"Well, well..." I stammered my way through, "I don't mean old as in OLD, you know..."

"Whadyu mean?" Ono Matapoeia said.

"What I mean is, everybody knows them already. They've been around for ages, I mean...a really long time."

"Have yuhevow banghed someone?" she said, seriously.

"WHAT?!"

Miss Mesmowize: "Have YOU ever BANGED someone?"

Were these people in their right minds?

"You know what? Forget about it." I gave up; whereupon Ono Matapoeia took the microphone and adjourned the meeting. Everyone was asked to stand and sing the anthem. The man in the shadows brought out his tabla and they threw themselves into a lustful rendition of *Ode to My Dictionary*.

Immediately they were done, a burly gentleman came over and introduced himself.

"Bro," he said, then pointing inwards with an easy and disarming smile, "John. Welcome to Compositions Anonymous. I'm from the House of Prose. Just wanted you to know that I appreciated your comment."

"Thanks," I said.

"See, folk here—this is the House of Poetry—don't get out much and hardly anyone visits, says, writes or knows anything about them so they believe that whatever they think up top"—he pointed to his temple, jabbing it repeatedly with his finger—"is all there is. Some of them were born in the room over there, believe me, man. This is their world, you know what I mean?"

"What about Ono Matapoeia? Where's she from?"

He laughed out loud.

"Brampton," he said. "And her name is Mata Poeia. Ono is just a title, like *Miss*. Got it?"

"I see."

In the corner of my eye, I sensed a shadow; and . . .

WHAM!

6. THE ONE-LEGGED TIGHTROPE WALKER
By Michael Joll

It was the summer of 1967, in Salamanca, Spain. I had a Ph.D. thesis to complete and defend the following January. A post-doc fellowship rode on the outcome.

My room in the medieval student hostel boasted the size and Spartan simplicity of a monk's cell, which it had probably been centuries ago when the building had been a monastery. After a three-second survey of my living quarters, I took in the view from my window. Four stories below, in the shade of an orange tree, a fountain guarded by four crouching stone lions gurgled in the flagstone courtyard. Across from my room, above Moorish arches, rose a similar building which, I guessed, housed the women students.

I made my way down the narrow, stone staircase and into the courtyard. A few students glanced up at my arrival, eyeing my long ponytail and Jesus beard. Or perhaps my beaded headband and a tie-dyed T-shirt tucked into faded bell-bottom jeans beneath my kaftan caught their attention. After a moment they turned away, the freak show over.

I blinked at the early afternoon sunlight before moving over to the shade of the orange tree and perched on the edge of the stone fountain. I let my fingers drift into the basin and swirl the water between them. Sweat trickled down my temples in the midsummer heat. I shrugged off my kaftan and placed it beside me.

A young woman detached herself from a group of students. She made her way over to the fountain and sat down beside me.

"*¿Americano?*" she said.

"Canadiense. ¿Y usted?"

"Islandesa. I'm from Reykjavik," she said in English. "I'm here for another two months, then back to Iceland to finish my degree. I've been here almost a year. I'm sick of nothing but Spanish all day, every day. Do you mind if we speak English?"

"Not at all."

"Guðrún Sigurdsdóttir," she said, holding out her hand. We shook formally. "My mother is American. My father is Iceland's ambassador to Spain. We speak English at home."

"Graydon Weston," I said. "From Toronto."

She returned my smile, then fell silent for several moments. I turned my attention to her thick blond hair pulled back in a ponytail, held in place at the nape by a black velvet bow. Very Tom Jones. Henry Fielding, not the singer. I snatched a glance at the upturned curve of her nose, her round eyes and high, delicate cheekbones. Small gold and pearl studs pierced the lobes of the pale shells of her ears. I was on the point of directing my examination to the enticing curves of her body when she fixed her blue-eyed gaze on my face.

"Why Salamanca?"

"I did my undergrad here. I'm completing my Ph.D. at the University of Toronto. I'm back doing some final research for my doctoral thesis, *Whither Spain after Franco?"*

"Bold. He's not dead yet and his legacy will cast a long, dark shadow."

"Y las parades oyen."

"You're right. Walls have ears, especially in Salamanca. This was Franco's first stronghold, and they're still very pro. Few are willing to speak openly, least of all to criticize the régime."

"I was aware of that. It's part of my thesis."

Guðrún's face froze and her body stiffened. She turned her back on me and edged away.

"I'm sorry," I said. "I didn't mean it to sound that way."

"But it did all the same," she snapped. "I'm just an undergrad. You've almost finished your Ph.D. But there's still no need to belittle me." She rose, and without looking back, rejoined her group of friends.

It was too late now to offer any explanation. Guðrún, I figured, had just ended our two-minute relationship. Any future with her did not look optimistic.

*

I spent my days and most of my evenings researching at the university and public libraries until my eyeballs felt like sandpaper. I wrote reams of notes until my wrist and fingers screamed at me to stop. I made no measurable progress on my thesis. I couldn't take my mind off Guðrún.

Despairing of my mental study block, I ventured into the empty courtyard one Sunday evening. A flock of small, chattering birds blasted away from the orange tree. Only the trickle of water from the fountain broke the silence that replaced them. A shadow stirred beneath an arch. Guðrún approached. She sat down beside me without saying a word. Several minutes later, she turned to me. I made to stand but she put her hand on my arm. "I saw you here alone. I'm sorry I spoke harshly before."

"It was my fault. I should have been more sensitive."

"How are the studies going?"

"They've ground to a halt. Zero progress. Nada. No karma. No muse. Maybe the moon is in the wrong house, or the stars are misaligned."

"This is the dawning of the Age of Aquarius."

"If only I knew what that meant."

Guðrún laughed. "I don't know either." She fell silent and splashed her fingers in the water. "These are uncertain times for Spain."

"If you will forgive the tired clichés, I expect the transition will be difficult, but the future will unfold, and Spain needs to be ready for it. That is the central thrust of my thesis."

"I hope you won't write it like that."

"I was thinking of using it as my opening sentence."

"Oh, God, if you do, no one will ever read past the first line. Even professors need something apart from coffee to keep them awake."

I laughed. "Too serious?"

"Totally. And banal."

"That bad, eh?"

"It will take more than a double espresso to stay awake. And the caffeine jolt will wear off in a heartbeat if the second sentence is as bad as the first."

"So, back to the drawing board?"

"I would advise it unless you want your thesis dismissed in the same way a treatise on pig husbandry would be in Saudi Arabia. Have you thought of putting a human face on it?"

"My thesis? No. It's supposed to be an academic analysis of the future of a country in transition and its options. I have my ideas based on my research, but, as you pointed out, I need an opening that won't cause the reader to fall into a coma."

Guðrún thought for a moment. "I know someone who may be willing to talk. He hates Franco. He's old, and I suspect he has little left to lose. He'll be suspicious of you, but he knows me. If you're careful and guarantee him anonymity, he might open up."

"I have to cite my sources, even if they are anecdotal, but I can change his name. Besides, I doubt if anyone on the review panel will check too closely."

"I'll set something up. How can I get hold of you?"

I pointed to my building. "Room four-o-four. You can leave a message at the front desk."

Guðrún rose and brushed her fingers against my arm. "I'll be in touch as soon as I have anything to report."

"You make it sound like a cloak and dagger assignment."

"In Spain, it is."

*

A week later we took the bus to a drab-looking bar in a dreary workers' quarter of Salamanca. Through the open door, over Guðrún's shoulder, I made out a row of silent drinkers standing belly up to the bar. When Guðrún brushed her way past them, the men turned as one and glowered at us with the sullen hostility reserved for intruders. I followed her to the only occupied table at the rear.

The man at the table looked to be in his sixties, or possibly older. When Guðrún stopped in front of him, he removed his beret but did not attempt to stand. A pair of simple, home-made wooden crutches lay propped against a chair beside him. A tear spilled from a vivid pink sty in one corner of an eye the colour of roast chestnuts and trickled down a furrow in his bristly cheek. He kept his grubby hands folded on the tabletop while he regarded me with suspicion.

"What do you want?"

I glanced at Guðrún and cleared my throat, but Guðrún placed her hand on my arm before I could speak. "Don Ignacio, my friend wants to ask you about your experiences in the war. If he writes about them, he will not mention your name or identify you in any way. You have nothing to fear. May we sit with you?"

"I fear no man, or his army, or his thugs and his henchmen," the old man said and hawked a gob of throat spittle onto the filthy floor.

"Your identity and what you tell me," I said, "will remain secret."

He stared at me as if sizing me up for trustworthiness. After a moment he nodded imperceptibly at Guðrún and turned to me. "I know Guðrún. That you are her friend and she vouches for you is enough for me to trust you. For now."

"Thank you."

"My name is Ignacio Saenz de Ferrán, and I drink Carlos Quinto if you're buying."

Guðrún rose and returned a few moments later with the bottle of brandy and three glasses.

"All I ever wanted to do was to play football," Don Ignacio said. "I was good, but never quite good enough to turn professional." He leaned forward confidentially. "And I was never any good at school. I hated it. I left as soon as I could. I hated Latin especially. Latin lessons always began with the same phrase—I will never forget it—*Discipuli picturam spectate.*"

"Students, look at the picture," I said.

"Exactly. Always the same. A drawing of the geese saving Rome, or Horatio defending the bridge, or some such nonsense. Then the story in Latin. My Latin master was a priest. I think it was in Latin class that I became an atheist." He snorted.

From the time he was fourteen, Don Ignacio said, he worked in his father's *pinchazería* in Salamanca, a hole-in-the-wall garage that specialized in repairing punctured inner tubes. He played football whenever he was not at work, and at eighteen, a club offered him an opportunity to play semi-professionally in Santander. At twenty-two, an injury followed by a botched operation, left the leg permanently fused at the knee. With his savings, he opened a *pinchazería* in Bilbao, but without business sense, the business struggled for years, until eventually, he went broke.

"It was the nineteen-thirties," he said. "Times were hard. I had no job. Nothing. I drifted to Madrid, then to Barcelona, looking for work. In Barcelona, a man approached me one day and asked if I could walk a tightrope. 'Of course,' I said, even though I had never walked a tightrope in my life. But it couldn't be hard. Other people did it. And it was a job. It paid money, not just a meal and a glass of wine."

He thought for a moment. "You know the Ramblas in Barcelona?"

I nodded.

"So, you know how wide it is."

"A hundred metres, at a guess."

"My job was to hang advertising from a rope suspended above the Ramblas. To do that I had to stand on a rope beneath that one. You can imagine, an arm full of cardboard letters one-metre square, balancing on a rope twenty metres above the street, fixing them to the rope above me which I could barely reach. I had no safety harness, no net, nothing. If I fell, I was dead. If I succeeded, I made a few hundred pesetas, enough to live on for a month." Don Ignacio leaned forward again. "As you can see, I succeeded."

"But how did you manage to walk a tightrope on only one leg?"

The old man uttered a guttural, phlegm-filled laugh that induced a wheeze. He gulped a mouthful of brandy and recovered his breath. "That came later. In the war."

I glanced surreptitiously at Guðrún and took a sip of my brandy. She looked away.

"By the time the civil war broke out I had a job mending holes in the roads back in Bilbao. It was not much, and I was lucky to have even that, with my leg stiff the way it was. I was not fit enough to join the anti-Franco forces and fight. But I did what I could. I worked with the underground. You didn't know there was a Spanish Resistance, did you?"

I shook my head.

"It was a big secret, but like all secrets, eventually word got out. Someone betrayed us. I escaped to Guérnica. You have heard of the place?"

I nodded.

"I met a young woman there. We planned to be married. Her mother had half a house in town. She said we could move in with her."

Don Ignacio paused for several moments before gulping his brandy. He wiped away a tear trickling down his cheek with the back of a grimy hand. "Guérnica was a symbol of the resistance to Franco. He had to teach it a lesson, one the townspeople, and the rest of Spain would never forget."

He took a final deep swallow of his brandy, poured another and cradled the glass in his hands. "I will never forget the date. In the afternoon of April twenty-sixth, nineteen thirty-seven, planes of the German Condor Legion, on the orders of the bastard Franco, bombed the defenceless town. They killed my fiancée and her mother and buried them in a mass grave without a marker. When they pulled me from the mound of rubble that was all that remained of the house, they had to amputate my leg, my good leg." He spat on the floor then finished his brandy in a single gulp. "I will never forgive them. Or forget."

Guðrún poured another brandy into his glass. He downed it in two swallows, then set the tumbler down hard on the tabletop.

"Now you know why I detest Franco," Don Ignacio snarled. A purple vein pulsed in his temple. He lowered his voice to a low growl. "For more than half my life I have hated Franco. I wish him dead. It cannot come soon enough. Only then will Spain be free again. It will be too late for the people of my generation, but we can hope that young people like you can grow up without living in fear."

He glanced around the room, but the drinkers at the bar seemed content to ignore us. "We cannot ask about the fate of those who disappeared during the war. We are branded as troublemakers. There are reprisals for those who do. We are silenced. Like those who disappeared in the war, we disappear too."

The old man leaned back and closed his eyes. He wiped a tear away with his shirtsleeve. Guðrún patted his arm. "Thank you for sharing this with us," she said quietly.

"I returned to Salamanca after the war," Don Ignacio said. "It was where I was born and grew up. My father was still here. In the end, he gave me a job. I have lived here ever since. From here I watched Europe go up in flames while Spain struggled under the heel of its own dictator. There are still old men like me in Salamanca, men who remember and do what they can to disrupt the Government. But we cannot do much except put up token resistance."

I raised an eyebrow.

He leaned forward and lowered his voice. "Petty vandalism. A *guardia civil* vehicle with a mysterious flat tire. One of their bicycles disappears for a few days. Little things to annoy the authorities." He laughed, heartily this time. "We have fun being naughty little boys." He closed his eyes. The interview had drawn to an end.

"We will leave you now." Guðrún stood and made her way towards the exit.

"Thank you, Don Ignacio," I said.

The old man grabbed my arm. His fingers dug into the flesh. "Be sure you tell the world."

"I will."

"But not about my small criminal activities, you understand. My grave will claim me one day, but I do not wish to disappear. Not yet." He stared at me and pursed his lips. "She is very pretty."

"I had noticed."

"And she likes you."

"How can you be so sure?"

"By how she looks at you. And touches your arm. Be good to her."

I blushed.

"There is one more thing," Don Ignacio said, eyeing me up and down.

"What is that?"

"You look ridiculous in those clothes."

I laughed and squeezed the old man's shoulder. I left Don Ignacio at his table with half the bottle of brandy. On my way to the door, a man stepped into my path. The murmur of voices at the bar ceased.

"It is lies, all lies," the man growled. "None of that happened." His eyes flitted around the room before they settled on Don Ignacio. The other men had their backs to me, staring deliberately ahead while studying the brief confrontation behind them through the mirror over the bar. The man glared at me, then stepped aside. The murmured voices resumed.

Outside the bar, Guðrún turned to me. "Did you believe him?"

"Don Ignacio? I'm not sure. He didn't say much about the Franco régime, but what he did divulge had the ring of truth about it."

"He told me the story once before, much the way he told it tonight, but without many of the details. That is why I wanted you to hear it for yourself. Can you use it in your thesis?"

I thought for a moment. "I'm not sure how it will fit into an academic thesis. It is more like an article in Paris Match or Life magazine."

"You could write it, though, couldn't you? It's an interesting story. It puts a human face onto Spain's recent past. It might provide an open doorway, a glimpse into Spain's future."

"Far better than my proposed opening paragraph. I may need some help with the more creative aspects."

We waited on the sidewalk for the bus. Our fingers touched. We squeezed hands. Guðrún slipped her arm through mine. I drew her against me, enjoying the uncomplicated silence, her warm body and her light perfume.

The bus arrived. We boarded and took seats at the rear, but before the bus could pull away a *guardia civil* van pulled up in front of it and boxed us in. Guðrún had her eyes closed, her head buried in my shoulder and her arm linked through mine. I watched as two officers in uniform left the van, placed their patent leather bicorn hats firmly on their heads, and strode purposefully into the bar. A minute later I stiffened when they re-emerged with Don Ignacio in handcuffs hopping between them. They bundled him into the back and threw his crutches in after him. The van drove off. No one came looking for us. Moments later, with a belch of foul-smelling, black diesel exhaust, our bus lurched away from the curb.

When the bus deposited us at the stop near the hostel, for a moment we stood in the darkness between two pools of light thrown by the streetlamps. I asked myself if I should tell Guðrún about Don Ignacio. She had a right to know. But she would only become upset. Who knew what she might do? If she complained to the authorities, the *guardia civil* might arrest us both as accomplices, or subversives, or conspirators. In Spain, one could never be sure, not while Franco was still around. I decided to hold my tongue. I have never been a brave man. This wasn't my fight, and I had no desire to experience the black hole of trial-free Spanish justice or implicate Guðrún.

"What are you thinking about?"

"Nothing," I said.

"I have a copy of the *Kama Sutra*." Guðrún looked away as if embarrassed at the confession. "Have you read it?"

"No," I said, trying to sound offhand while a shot of adrenalin kick-started my imagination.

"If the authorities found it they would throw me in prison. I have diplomatic immunity, but you know how the Spanish are. They'd deny they knew anything about me, then take three days to *find* me." She made air quotes with her fingers. "I have my own apartment." She turned her head to face me. "We could study together if you like. I could help with creativity."

"I'd like that."

She stood on tiptoes and kissed me. "It's an Icelandic translation, but it's illustrated if you need help following the text."

The next morning, I shaved off my beard and had Guðrún cut my hair short. I bought some new clothes that afternoon and ditched the old ones.

When she asked why I had, I didn't tell her I needed to become invisible in Franco's Spain. "Don Ignacio said I look ridiculous."

*

When Guðrún died last year, I decided to downsize, starting with a lifetime's accumulation of books. But her copy of *Kama Sutra* stayed on the shelf.

7. THE MAN OF THE HOUSE

[1st PRIZE NON-FICTION BWG 2020 COMPETITION]

By Raymond Holmes

Anger smouldered in me on that July morning in 1954.

Mom said I had to come home—Summer vacation cut short for no reason. She'd find out how angry I was. After a boring journey, the train pulled into Toronto's Union Station. My empty stomach rattled.

"You get off here," said the conductor.

After descending to the platform with my small suitcase, I observed three people waving in the distance. I thought they were attracting another person's attention, but as they drew nearer, I realized that it was my mother, older sister and her husband, Harry.

"Why—?" I said before Sis burst out crying.

"Your father's gone," she said, blubbering through tears.

"Gone where?" I said.

"Daddy's passed away," Mother said in a quiet voice, her face ashen and eyes red.

I still didn't understand. Harry knelt down, grabbed my shoulders and looked me straight in the face. His breath reeked of beer.

"Your father died yesterday. Be strong for your mother." His words hung in the air and then careened through my mind like a flock of startled birds.

I stared at his slack face and dull eyes, letting the words soak in before running into my mother's arms howling. That set her and Sis off as well and the three of us stood on the train platform bawling. Harry didn't cry. He'd been a soldier in the war and those guys didn't cry for anything. People passing by smiled at us. A happy family reunion, they assumed.

Mother rubbed the back of my head as I kept wailing. I knew what death was: the pet goldfish floating belly up in its bowl or the lifeless cat in the gutter that didn't make it across our busy street, but they were animals. The idea of that happening to my father shocked and horrified me. It couldn't be. A week ago, we played catch in the back yard. He cut customers' hair in his barber shop the day I left.

"Have a good time. Catch a fish," he said and passed me spending-money.

No one spoke on the drive home. A feeling of despair overlaid with a kaleidoscope of emotions played inside me. I stared out the car window. Memories flashed. Apprehension for the future hovered like a black vulture. I couldn't believe I'd never see my father alive again.

We entered our home, walking through Dad's barber shop to the living quarters at the rear. Hoping this might be a cruel joke, I waited for my father to emerge and surprise me from the basement or the stairs leading down from the second floor.

That didn't happen.

The house remained quiet for the rest of the day except for customers' rattling the locked barbershop front door. Why wouldn't they leave us alone?

"Tomorrow we have to go to the funeral home to finalize Dad's arrangements," Mom said before dinner. I've never forgotten that word *arrangements*: the polite way of referring to the disposition of a deceased human being—an innocent, yet repulsive word.

"I've had your suit cleaned. It might be a little tight, but will do for now," she said.

"I don't want to go there," I told her.

"You have to. You're the man of the house now and must be there for your father." She opened the newspaper to the obituaries page and pointed to the one about Dad. I sensed she wanted me to see the printed words—accept the finality of his death.

At dinnertime, I stared at the kitchen door leading to the barber shop. Dad always came in, turned on the radio and said, "What's for dinner?"

"The World at Six," the radio news announcer said in a cheerful voice. I didn't care about the rest of the world. What would become of ours?

"Daddy dropped dead coming down the stairs," Mom said. "He was sick but didn't want anyone to know and worked right up to the end although I begged him not to. He died on his feet. I don't know how he did it."

"I wish I'd been here with you," I said in a squeaky voice before a storm of tears choked it off. We cried and hugged each other in the kitchen.

"I'm glad you weren't here," Mom said.

In bed that evening I tossed, turned and cried. A future without my father seemed like a dark tunnel I couldn't see the end of.

I could hear Mom weeping in the kitchen downstairs. I opened my door a crack and heard her praying. My mother was a strong woman. I knew things must be terrible if she was talking to God.

I lay awake for a long time. After falling asleep I dreamed my mother and sister had also died and I was left alone. In that tormenting nightmare their faces receded into the distance, their voices called my name and saying "goodbye," over and over. What would happen to me now?

When I awoke the next morning a joyless, barren feeling crawled into me and I shivered. Events of the previous day and the nightmare fluttered in my mind.

The sound of footsteps approached. Mom came into my bedroom and sat down on the edge of the bed, her face white and drawn, unkempt hair pulled back.

"You okay?" she said.

I wanted to release many feelings, but only said, "Yes."

"It's time to get up. We have a busy day today. Breakfast is on the table."

She left and I lay in bed staring at the ceiling, tears flooding the corners of my eyes.

"Come—now," she called a few minutes later.

I had no appetite.

After breakfast I went into Dad's barber shop. A fresh, white smock lay on his barber chair waiting for the owner who would never wear it again. A razor, comb, and clippers rested in a neat row on the counter ready for hands that could never use them. Morning sun passing through bottles of after-shave lotion on the counter splashed a rainbow of colours on the wall that reminded me of the windows at church. The clock on the wall ticked off seconds of life.

The trousers of my ill-fitting suit pressed into my waist and the black dress shoes pinched my feet during the four-block walk to the funeral home. A pale, gaunt funeral director greeted us. He reminded me of a ghoul. A heavy silence pervaded the building. A shudder strummed through my body like the string of an instrument which had been plucked with a giant finger.

"We're sorry for your loss," the stone-faced man said in an emotionless voice before glancing down at me. "What might this young master's name be?"

Intimidated, I didn't answer. Mother told him my name which he repeated. A crooked smile crossed his face.

"This way please," he said, pointing to a room on the right.

A sign near the door bore my father's name. Mom took me by the hand, and we walked up to the front of the room. Shivers ran up my legs and down my arms. She put her arm around my shoulder as we approached the casket. "Here's Daddy," she said.

The funeral director brought a stool and placed it alongside the silk-lined, polished oak casket with bright, gold-coloured handles fastened to the sides. The casket, sitting on a trolley, reminded me of a fancy bed. Bouquets of flowers on stands flanked both sides.

"Look," Mom said, pointing to an arrangement of red and white roses with an attached banner labelled SON. "That's from you." Banners on other bouquets of fragrant, colourful flowers read WIFE, DAUGHTER and BROTHER.

I stepped on the stool to look at my father. He was dressed in a blue, pin-striped double-breasted suit with a white shirt and knotted tie. He appeared to be asleep and I imagined at any moment he'd open his eyes, look at me and smile. His head, with neatly combed hair, rested on a pillow and his hands lay one atop the other on his chest. I noticed the waxy appearance of his face—expressionless, but peaceful. It looked different from the father I knew.

Only this still, lifeless form remained of the father I loved? My heart ached and vague fears clawed at me. My first experience of death. Where did you go when you died?

My mother stared into the casket, moving her head from side to side, right hand covering her mouth. "Touch Daddy's hand," she said.

I didn't want to. Her right hand pressed into my shoulder. "It's okay. Your father's sleeping in God's arms," she said, touching his left hand bearing a wedding ring on the third finger.

I touched his hand. The icy chill of death drew the warmth from my palm, and I pulled away.

As we turned from the coffin, the funeral director asked my mother to come to his office to sign papers. She nodded. I saw the troubled look on her face.

"The funeral costs a lot of money. I'll have to make monthly payments for two years," she said on the way home. I knew we didn't have much money. Mom and Dad had argued about bills arriving in the mail.

The next day at the visitation, a hum of voices filled the room. Many of Dad's customers came to pay their respects. I recognized the owners of the drug store and restaurant near our home. People signed the blue, felt-covered visitor's book with gold lettering.

I sat in a chair watching people come and go. Relatives I'd never met introduced themselves. I forgot their names moments later. Strangers asked me stupid questions and made silly comments.

"Do you miss your father?"

"You loved your dad, didn't you?"

"How do you feel?"

"You're the man of the house now, y'know."

Mom said that too. What did it mean?

People walked up to Dad's casket with a mournful look on their faces and shook their heads.

"The funeral home does them up nice, don't they?"

"Jimmy's at rest now. He had a good life."

Dad just cut their hair. How could they know about his life? Memories of my father rushed through my mind: playing board games after dinner, drives in the car, learning to fish.

A man gave me money and Mom said to go to the variety store across the street and buy myself a treat. "It's difficult for a young child to be cooped up in here," I overheard her say to a neighbour. I felt guilty about being bored and treating myself when my father was dead. I walked to and from the store in a daze and don't remember what I bought.

"My legs and back ache from standing and I'm tired of talking to people," Mom said as we left the funeral home after the visitation.

At the funeral service the next day a woman played *Abide With Me* on the organ—Mom's favourite hymn. Dad didn't attend church. The wooden chair numbed my backside and my underarms oozed perspiration. The bald minister with silver-rimmed spectacles spoke for a long time. He said how my father had touched many lives and as a barber, many heads as well. People laughed. Why was that funny?

"One day our hearts will stop and we will die," he said. "Leave here resolved to use every day of your life well."

Goosebumps erupted on my arms. My own death was far in the future and remote. I didn't want to think about it. Those last instructions from the minister have always haunted me. Has my life been well spent?

At the cemetery, rain fell off the edges of umbrellas surrounding the grave site like water spilling off a patch of black mushrooms.

The minister quoted a bible passage. "To everything there is a season..." At the end he said, "Ashes to ashes, dust to dust."

Mom laid two red roses on the casket and then wiped her eyes with a tissue crumpled in her hand. I started to cry. That action said "goodbye forever" as a last gesture of love that no words could. A woman nearby crossed herself. My sister sobbed. Two men lowered the heavy casket into the ground. They dumped the baskets of withering flowers in a pile beside the grave. The thought of being buried in the earth filled me with horror.

When we arrived home the silence in the house made it seem as if the world had stopped. Death, the thief, had entered and stolen my father. My friends still had fathers and I didn't. What would I say to them? I went upstairs, sprawled on my bed and cried.

Mom came up, sat down beside me and rubbed my back.

"There's just the two of us now," she said.

"I'm afraid," I told her.

"Why?"

"Of what will happen now that Dad's not here." I was also fearful that she might die but didn't say that.

"Life has to go on. You and I have each other and will share what we have. Things will be fine—you'll see."

"I miss Dad."

"So do I. We won't forget him. He'll always live in our hearts."

She reached into her apron pocket. "This is for you."

Dad's pocket watch rested in her open palm.

"He wanted you to have it," she said.

I had always admired that watch and asked to see it many times. The case had a transparent back which displayed the operating movement. It would forever be a part of my father and in my hand seemed to radiate warmth.

I looked at my mother's tender, kind face. Her love would enable me to feel secure enough to face the future. I vowed to be a good, loving son in return, but there was more anguish in store for her at the end of the month. Bill collectors harassed her for money Dad owed. The landlord asked if we were staying and when Mom said yes, he raised the rent by five dollars per month. We lived in a heartless world that kicked people when they were down.

One evening in mid-August Mom laughed while listening to the Jack Benny Program on the radio, amused by the pregnant pauses in his dialogue with Rochester and his exasperated comments including, "Well—" and "Now cut that out!"

Who remembers an episode of laughter on an evening more than sixty-five years ago? It was the first time my mother had laughed since Dad's death and did so in a hearty fashion that illuminated her face with pleasure. I felt a lightness rise in me and smiled at that first happy interlude in our sorrowful existence since Dad's funeral.

Grief would pass slowly from our lives, but it was a burden we eventually laid down.

8. BABY SHOES

By Rena Flannigan

Ernest Hemingway was challenged to a write a short story of less than six words; this is what he wrote "For Sale, Baby Shoes, Never Worn."

I am not selling my baby's shoes—they hold too many memories for me. They are sitting on my desk as I try to remember all the cute things my children did while wearing them. It is hard to think back fifty-eight years though. Because I am a sentimental and thrifty person, I kept the shoes after my son Stewart outgrew them and my daughter Ingrid, wore them five years after he did. I put little bells on the laces, so it was like Christmas, as every time they walked or attempted to run, I heard the bells ringing and I knew they were on their way to Mummy. A beautiful time of my life, and I loved being their mother.

Of all the joys I have been lucky enough to have, at times being a mother was the best of the best. I was at a point in my life when I thought I would never have children and I wanted them so much. I am a baby person but not, as it happened, a baby-making machine. I like to think I am a loving person and to give children, especially my own, loads of love would have pleased me no end.

What about the shoes? Not much except I can see my toddler in his nice clothes and even in his *lederhosen* (German shorts), which he hated wearing. Despite my appealing to his understanding of how good it was to know he could not do any damage to them playing in the dirt and so on. Besides, he would make it easier for me when it came to laundry—I would not have as many clothes to wash, I told him. Maybe this is why he never forgave me in later years for making him wear the blasted things—only to appease other people. He outgrew them and I gave them to my Austrian neighbours across the road. They were still very much into the culture of their old country. It was handy having these neighbours because as my son outgrew his clothes their little boy got them. They were all of good quality and it was great to have someone we knew who could use them.

My husband was Austrian, I am a Scot. My aunt sent me some tartan material to make a kilt for my son. I had to explain to her that a kilt would be the last thing he would ever wear, even as a child. I used the Stewart tartan material she had sent to make myself an evening gown.

Ah yes, the shoes. Standing all dressed up and wearing his shoes my son looked adorable. How could I not love this wonderful child I had given birth to? One thing that stands out in memory was the day he stood in his bedroom doorway and showed me how he had closed a safety pin. He held it up so proudly. In those days, we used cloth diapers which had to be fastened with safety pins. I still have some of them, blue for boys and pink for girls. He was quite small when he closed the pin so naturally Mummy was very proud of him and hugged him tightly. I called him a Clever Darling most of his life; he developed into a capable and excellent worker able to do so many things.

Five years after my son was born, I was blessed with a beautiful daughter who has been my mainstay for so much of her life. When she was little and I was going through some rough patches I would say to her, "Give Mummy one of your wonderful hugs, Darling." She did and I felt so much of my tension dropping away. Even today, fifty-three years later, her hugs still have that magic in them. She too had so many lovely outfits to wear, including her *Dirndls*. She was a small version of a fraulein with her golden curls. She looked adorable, and she wore the same shoes. Now I have them beside me and I think back on all the years gone by. I only wish I could recall many more things. Too many years and so much of life have passed. My Austrian neighbours had a little girl after my daughter was born so she inherited my daughter's lovely clothes—but not the shoes.

My mother worked as a cashier in the basement cafeteria of the Eaton Annex, and from time to time I would meet her there and rummage through the children's department where there were lots of good items at sale prices. One day I picked up a snowsuit for my son, paying the princely sum of three dollars for it. A great bargain to begin with and to think: four children wore it until they all outgrew it. My son wore it, then across the road it went where the little boy there outgrew it. Back to me for my daughter until she could barely get into it and once more across the street it went until the other little girl grew too big for it. An amazing three-dollar bargain.

As the children grew bigger the snowsuit occasionally came apart at the seams and this is where my talents entered the fray. Having been a seamstress for most of my life, I knew how to take the garment apart, fix it and sew it up again. Talent comes in handy at times. Those little shoes were going from son to daughter. Even all these years later they are still in fairly good condition, but my daughter did not use them for any of her children. My granddaughter would not use them either, not modern enough for anyone today, I suppose.

I would not part with them, in any case. They hold so many lovely recollections in my memory, particularly the day my son fastened the safety pin. Strange thing to remember I know, but one memory I hope I keep in my mind and heart till my dying day.

The last footwear my son wore was military boots when he was in the navy. They shone like a mirror. He is gone now; pancreatic cancer took him at age fifty-five. He was a Thanksgiving baby, ironic that he died a month before Thanksgiving. What I now have are the memories of him in his baby shoes.

I am so happy I still have my beautiful daughter to love—she tells me I love her too much—how could I not? And I remember when she also wore the shoes.

I wonder if Hemmingway ever sold the shoes in his six-word story. My story is a little longer and even if I was offered a billion dollars (prices being so inflated now!) I would not part with the precious shoes of my children.

No matter how shoe fashions come and go, none will ever replace my baby shoes.

9. WOVEN TOGETHER

[3rd PRIZE NON-FICTION BWG 2020 COMPETITION]
By CHERRY NARULA

Worldwide, there are over 476 million Indigenous peoples in more than 90 countries, representing 5,000 d+ifferent cultures who speak a majority of the world's estimated 7,000 languages. These diverse and dynamic societies maintain the traditions of the original culture of their region.

International Day of the World's Indigenous Peoples is commemorated on August 9th every year to raise awareness of the needs of these people. Despite practicing unique and varied cultures, many of their problems are similar and their traditional lifestyle has been a source of resilience in this journey of seeking recognition for their way of life and their identities.

Indigenous peoples consider nature sacred and know how to take care of it. Their deep respect for nature sustains ways of life that enhance knowledge of nature conservation and use of natural resources. Indigenous perspectives can aid conservation efforts and increase biodiversity sustainment through traditional practices. These practices are also essential to ensure that species survive and thrive. It is key to understand and recognise Indigenous relationships to the environment by learning and working together in preservation efforts. Indigenous communities are ideal custodians of ecosystems and are vital for a better world.

Throughout history, Indigenous peoples have been subjected to violations of their rights and as the United Nations and governments worldwide work towards restoring the rights of Indigenous peoples, we can help by appreciating and recognising their culture and wisdom. Each of the 5,000 diverse Indigenous cultures worldwide have their own unique history and traditions. In British Columbia alone there are over 200 First Nation communities, each one having its own uniquely diverse culture and language. Canada is home to about 1.7 million Indigenous peoples. Similarly, in another part of the world, in India there are over 104 million Indigenous peoples. While appreciating the fabric of two diverse cultures in two different continents, there is an impression of a weave running through one end of the world to the other. Despite being culturally distinct societies and communities, a common spirit of shared values becomes evident frequently.

In North America, Coast Salish peoples are a grouping of Indigenous peoples with several different cultures and languages and their dynamic and diverse culture includes a number of First Nations who are inextricably bound to land and natural resources. This connection also constitutes the basis of the physical and spiritual well-being of people who have mostly lived in the territories along the Northwest Pacific Coast comprising of parts of Washington and Oregon states in the United States and the province of British Columbia in Canada. In British Columbia, this includes the ecologically diverse Strait of Georgia, Puget Sound and Strait of Juan de Fuca, also known as the Salish sea. The Strait of Georgia itself is one of the world's most biologically productive marine ecosystems having a large variety of marine habitats that support about 3,000 species of marine life, making the Coast Salish fisheries well known across the globe.

Historically, Coast Salish peoples have lived in permanent villages during the winter and in temporary camps in the summer while gathering food. They are well known for their beautiful and unique art—their creations centered on story-telling and spirituality. They use Totem poles as a traditional way of telling their stories by commemorating family history, ancestry, or events, and these are mostly carved out of red cedar and painted in vibrant colours. Totem poles come alive when the stories related to their crests are known and the crests tell the story of the family to whom they belong. These stories serve to document important events and family histories. Wealthy families may have more than one crest to mark the family's lineage. Traditionally, Coast Salish peoples have also carved house posts to feature animals and spiritual beings— the carved planks used both on the interior and exterior of their ceremonial houses. The artistic life of the Coast Salish peoples brings to life sculptures, paintings, robes, blankets, and woven baskets.

Salish culture is renowned for the art of weaving and the use of the spindle whorl. The womenfolk are responsible for making blankets and girls train with their grandmothers at a very young age to carry on the legacy. They are renowned skilled weavers of the Pacific Northwest, famous for their beautiful twill blankets. Salish blankets were used as currency to purchase goods and were given to other villages as a sign of prosperity of the community or individual presenting it. These were also presented to honour members of the community. These are still used as a mark of status and protection in ceremonies. Salish blankets are considered protective garments of powerful spiritual significance, offering focus and strength during life changing events.

The Coast Salish spindle whorls are known for their exceptional carved geometric, human, or animal designs. The loom is made of two vertical posts supported by two horizontal bars. The blankets are woven on those bars. The vertical posts are used for making adjustments and variations. Coast Salish peoples have used weaving materials found locally, such as cedar bark, willow bark, nettle fibre, milkweed fibre, mountain goat's wool, and woolly dog's hair. Shredded cedar bark twisted with wool of mountain goats has been used to form the warp. Their legacy includes twined mountain goat wool robes, twill-plaited blankets in geometric designs made of goat wool, cattail fluff, as well as dog wool sheared from small woolly dogs. Salish wool was mostly created by mixing goat and dog wool. The white wool of the mountain goat is the most revered fibre for Coast Salish peoples. The mountain goat is considered the purest of all animals since it lives in remote areas with a proximity to the sky. However, these days, domestic sheep wool is mostly used by Coast Salish weavers.

Weaving cattail mats and baskets were also an important part of daily life. Women sewed cattail leaves together to make large mats used for shelters, dividers, insulation, kneeling pads, and sleeping mats. Similarly, baskets were used in almost every area of daily life. Coiled, twined, or plaited baskets were used for regular household chores. Baskets were used for gathering, storing, and preparing food, storing household goods, transporting objects, and protecting infants. Coiled baskets made of cedar roots were tight enough to boil soups. Twined baskets made of materials that include cattail leaves, spruce roots and cedar bark were more pliable and softer than coiled baskets. Utility baskets were mostly made of split cedar bark and grass by both plaiting and twining techniques. Some baskets were decorated with motifs and geometric patterns made from materials such as dyed cedar bark, bear grass, or horsetail rhizomes. Painted designs also decorated some baskets on the outside. Colours and dyes were created from plants and natural mineral sources.

On the other side of the world, in Asia, the Indigenous peoples of the mountain frontier between India and Burma are called Nagas. They belong to about 66 different tribes that have a population of approximately 3.5 million. Nagas constitute various ethnic groups that are native to northeastern India and northwestern Myanmar. In India, Naga tribes reside in the northeastern states of Nagaland, Manipur, Assam, and Arunachal Pradesh. Traditionally, Nagas established their settlements on hilltops and mountains to defend themselves from neighbouring tribes. The Naga villages were designed to be self-sufficient and secure and they have a great understanding of the wildlife that surrounds them. Their legends depict humans and animals exchanging roles and providing for one another and this interrelationship with the animal world is reflected in the Naga artwork.

Majority of the Naga tribes call Nagaland home where about 2 million Nagas belonging to sixteen major tribes live. The Nagas believe in the oneness and harmony with their environment.

Nagaland is primarily a mountainous state with the Naga Hills emerging from the Brahmaputra valley in Assam. The tributaries of one of the world's largest rivers, the Brahmaputra, criss-crosses the terrain. This land is rich in rain forests with unique flora and fauna. The evergreen tropical and sub-tropical forests have a rich foliage of bamboo, palm, rattan, timber, and mahogany forests with more than 490 species of birds and 396 species of orchids out of which some have importance for horticultural and medicinal purposes. Nagaland also has an abundance of natural stone and mineral reserves such as marble, limestone, chromium, coal, cobalt, iron, and nickel. This terrain is a part of a complex mountain system that has been declared a *National Geological Monument of India.*

Nagaland is also known for its terraced paddy fields. Naga tribes still carve the hillsides by hand, using their traditional methods. The Indigenous system of paddy cultivation has been used to bring back to life deserted barren fields. A network of water channels irrigates the paddy terraces, with bamboo pipes being used at times to regulate the water flow. This terraced paddy cultivation, hand carved on hillsides, is a great visual treat. Jute and cotton are also commonly cultivated to complement the rich Naga tradition of art and craft. Weaving is a traditional art of the Nagas that has been handed down through generations. The art of weaving and wearing the traditional dress is linked to several diverse traditions and beliefs. The colour combination, pattern and design symbolise a specific tribe and status in society. Each Naga tribe has its unique textile heritage with distinct motifs and designs.

The Nagas are best known for their shawls. The traditional use of yarn and natural dyes makes the Naga textiles unique. The women folk mostly are engaged in the spinning of textiles. Little girls can be seen experimenting with weaving while playing with toy looms. In these remote misty mountains, Naga women can still be seen on the hillsides using their traditional backstrap looms. The Naga loom is a simple backstrap loom, also called the lion loom that is adjustable to the body of the weaver. The lion loom is a simple, low-cost, portable loom that uses two parallel bamboos to stretch the warp yarn. One end is fixed to a post or wall and the other end is held steady by a strap around the waist of the weaver. Weaving techniques have been perfected over the centuries to allow a single weaver to weave wider fabrics in less time. This led to the creation of the fly shuttle loom to weave wider fabrics in larger quantities. Traditional shawl weaving is still done on the lion looms while fabrics are woven on the fly shuttle loom. Natural dyes extracted from plants, barks, and roots are used for textile dyeing.

Another distinctive Naga craft is the bamboo craft. Bamboo is extensively used in daily life. Furniture, baskets, mats, cups, utensils, or musical instruments like mouth organ, flute, and trumpet are all made of bamboo. Nagas also take great pride in their tradition of basket weaving. Each Naga tribe has a distinct style of basketry. Traditionally every Naga man was a bamboo craftsman. This was a skill that a young boy would pick up from his elders. Backpacks made of cane were used for hunting. Baskets made of cane and bamboo were used to fetch water and collect harvest. Baskets continue to be used for storage and for carrying essential items, small children, or livestock. Even today, mostly men weave baskets and their first gift to their beloved is an intricately woven basket as a symbol of their commitment.

Despite the ethnic and cultural differences between Indigenous peoples all over the world, there are some striking similarities. These similarities stem from their deep relationship to the environment, land, and natural resources. Each aspect of their lives is inseparable from the natural world. Their stories and ceremonies are a constant reminder to them of their sacred duty to protect the environment. Many of their beliefs and superstitions can be linked to deep truths and profound philosophies. There is an interconnectedness that runs through the spirit of learning from the past and utilising Indigenous methods to protect historical sites, wildlife, and the environment.

Each Indigenous culture is unique and distinct from the dominant societies in which they live today. When we do not make the effort to learn about indigenous cultures, we fail to understand the value of their practices and way of life. Their remarkable culture and way of life must be recognised, understood, and protected. The United Nations has been working to strengthen international cooperation for solving the problems faced by Indigenous peoples worldwide. A new decade for the Indigenous community begins next year with the celebration of the *Decade of Indigenous Languages 2022 – 2032*. The Indigenous peoples play an important role in sustaining the diversity of the world's biological and cultural landscape. Traditional values and knowledge systems must be maintained and passed on to future generations. The rich cultural history and the unique system of Indigenous beliefs that have been passed from the remote past are vital for the future well-being of the world.

<u>Bibliography</u>

Encyclopedia.com. (2020, September 24). Naga.
https://www.encyclopedia.com/philosophy-and-religion/eastern-religions/buddhism/naga

Government of Canada. (2020. September 23). Indigenous peoples.
https://www.canada.ca/en/services/indigenous-peoples.html

Kennedy, D., & Bouchard, R. (2006, February 7). Coast Salish.
https://www.thecanadianencyclopedia.ca/en/article/coastal-salish

The World Bank IBRD IDA. (2020, September 24). Indigenous Peoples.
https://www.worldbank.org/en/topic/indigenouspeoples

UNESCO. (2020, January 08). Indigenous Peoples.
https://en.unesco.org/indigenous-peoples

United Nations. (2020, August 9). International Day of the World's Indigenous Peoples. https://www.un.org/en/observances/indigenous-day

10.   BEST BEFORE

By Ken Puddicombe

The table had been set, the wine poured, the turkey carved, and Cutie was hoping they would have a peaceful dinner, for a change.

She had put up with Rommel's bickering and moaning for over twenty years, not only her, but their son Quince, the boy more so, in whom she saw growing signs of frustation. They were both tired of hearing the same lament, an unceasing barrage of complaints about life in Canada—the cold winters, hot summers, and everything in-between.

Rommel reached over for the platter with the turkey and paused before he filled his plate. "Of course," he said, "back in Guyana, we'd be having ham instead of turkey. Those were the days. Can you remember the Christmas in our first house, Cutie?"

She glanced Quince who sighed, clearly exasperated hearing his father go on again about his boyhood days in the *colony with the highest standard of education in the Caribbean, when Georgetown was called the Garden City of the West Indies.*

Rommel had taken his position at the head of the table, as was customary on Christmas day. Cutie's place was at the opposite end, with faster access to the kitchen, Quince to the right of his father.

"Yes, Rommel, I remember," she said.

"Of course, that was long before you were born," Rommel said to Quince.

Rommel reached over for the wine decanter and filled his glass. "And we'd be having ginger-beer or sorrel drink instead of wine, garlic pork as a side dish, blackcake for desert instead of apple pie. Yes sir, those were the days."

Quince sucked his teeth but it was undetected in the midst of Rommel's noisy scooping of the turkey from the glass platter.

"Later on Christmas day, we'd wander over to the neighbour and partake of their food and have a drink, perhaps more sorrel As we grew older, we graduated to high wine or rum." Rommel sighed. "Can't do that today. Too damn cold. Too much snow outside. Besides, how many people do you really know living on this street, anyhow? And even if you did know them, do you think you can hop over and have a drink with them? They would think you gone crazy.

"I know what you're going to say Quince. And I know you've heard it all before, but your childhood was a piece of cake compared to mine."

"Those days are long gone," Quince said. "They're not coming back, Dad. Can't you see that *Home* is here, now, in Canada."

"Home is where you born, boy. It's in the blood, in the DNA, yours and mine."

"You're forgetting Dad. You and mum were born there, I wasn't. So much for DNA, then."

"You still have a connection with the old country, boy, through me. It's a link that can never be broken."

"Well, I wish you'd stop talking about it. Why don't you *do* something about it?"

"But I will. It's the reason I built the house on the empty lot of land I bought when we were there. We should all go back, get away from this rat race."

Quince pushed his chair back and rose. "I can't speak for mum. But I'm never going back. It's too backward. Once was enough. You can go if you want, but don't plan on me joining you."

Quince headed for the foyer, picked his coat off the stand and went out to the driveway.

"Where's he going?" Rommel said. "It's Christmas day. Family time."

Cutie said, "He's going over to his girl to spend time with her."

"What's it now when a family can't have complete Christmas dinner and a relaxing evening together?"

"He's young. He's got a life of his own."

She pulled out an envelope from where it had been consigned under her place mat and turned it over to Rommel. "Merry Christmas."

He took the envelope, puzzled. "But we already open Christmas presents this morning."

"I know. It's just something else I got you."

The envelope was a half-size brown manilla, the flap tucked into the body.

He flipped it open and extracted a Christmas card. *To my husband. With best wishes for the years to come* printed on the front. Below the inscription, she'd written: "*Best Before January 31, 2000*". He opened the card and something fell on the table.

Enclosed in blue wrapping paper was an airline ticket. He smiled. "Oh, we going on vacation?" He took a closer look. "Ticket for Guyana. Sounds even better." Then his smile disappeared. "But it's only for me, Cutie!"

She nodded.

"Aren't you coming with me?"

She shook her head. "No Rommel. I'm giving you the chance to do what you've been dreaming of for so long."

"I don't understand. The house is built. It's why we've been sending money all these years, to go back and retire there."

There had been discussions and debates, all ending up in arguments when he raised the idea of building on the land he'd bought ten blocks from Lady's house on Independence Boulevard. It was *his* money, after all, that he sent to his sister for the project—a settlement for twenty-five years service, after which he was laid off from Northern.

"It's *your* dream, Rommel. I might come to visit you sometime. I can't say right now. But I think you should go, even if it's to get it out of your system." She wanted to add: *I'm looking forward to not hearing you hassle me about it all the time.* But she didn't. It was Christmas.

"But I'm telling you, we can make it work. The house is completed— you've' seen the pictures that Lady sent. It's got all the conveniences we have here. It will be just like the old days, I tell you, even better."

Rommel pulled out a photograph from the inside pocket of his blazer and looked at it. He smiled. He'd started carrying that picture around with him since his sister sent it last year. The house looked splendid. A concrete structure, two floors, a verandah in front to catch the north-easterly sweeping in from the Atlantic, all surrounded by a high chain-link fence. Enough land at the rear for a vegetable garden. His sister had said it was the jewel of Independence Boulevard, the envy of the neighbourhood.

"I suppose you're right. Only time will tell. I'm hoping you will change your mind once I'm there, and join me," he said.

*

Rommel came out of the terminal pulling his suitcase, his old BWIA carry-on slung over his right shoulder.

At the end of a queue, he had to surrender his luggage ticket to two armed guards who compared the serial number with that on the suitcase and let him go. These were not the only armed guards he'd seen since arriving. They were spread throughout the terminal.

A tall Black man hailed him. "Heading for GT man? I can tekh you." The man attempted to grab his suitcase and he resisted. Someone grabbing his suitcase was not the right type of person to give his business.

The hand-written sign- INDEPENDENCE BOULEVARD, written in black, bold letters, was up high at the rear of the crowd and he stopped short and doubled back to see who was holding it.

The man, about five feet three in height, was the shortest in the batch of taxi drivers crammed outside the arrivals area.

"You're going to Independence Boulevard?" Rommel said.

"Yes boss. I can tekh you there."

The man led the way out the terminal to the parking lot.

"And your name is?"

"Babooram, but you can call me Ram. Ah live right on Independence Boulevard, boss. I know it well."

"Before we go. How much is this going to cost me?"

"Not much boss. You got US or Canadian?"

"Canadian."

"How about if we settle for twenty-five? Tip included."

Ram placed the suitcase in the trunk of the old Morris Oxford and strapped the lid with rope. He opened the left door to the front and closed it behind Rommel, then took his place behind the wheel.

Rommel looked around the car, up and over, and to his right.

Ram laughed. "Don' worry looking for seat belt, boss. The car got none. Besides, we in Guyana, you know. So you not breaking the law."

Ram turned the key in the ignition and the car sputtered to life. He took a careful look at his passenger before he pulled out of the parking lot. "You got a knowing face. Didn't you and your family live down by the Well Road off Independence Boulevard?"

"As a matter of fact, we did. That was way back in the fifties, before I left Guyana."

They left the airport behind and headed north on the single lane highway. A steady stream of traffic came in the opposite direction.

"Lots of traffic—are they all heading to the airport?"

Ram nodded. "Yes, but they early for the morning flight back to Toronto." Ram glanced in the rearview mirror. "How long you been away?"

"I left in nineteen sixty-four."

"And you never been back?"

"Once, briefly for a two-week vacation in 1980."

"Well, is a lot of changes in the country since then, some good, some bad."

"What's good?"

"Lots of money coming in from people like you coming back to take up residence. Building booming. Lots of people trading. The economy is growing fast, fast."

Rommel smiled. It was as he expected. "So, tell me about the bad, now."

Ram passed his left hand slowly across his scalp. He was practically bald, apart for a tuft of hair growing at the sides of his head.

"A lot of fraud. You still can't get something done without greasing somebody's palm in government. And crime increase, big, big time."

"I guess it's not much different from any developing country."

Ram shrugged. "Except, drug smuggling is a big t'ing, too." He laughed. "You just have to look at the big houses in Georgetown and ask yourself where the money coming from."

As they drove down the road, Rommel was amazed at the number of young people hanging around the bars, drinking and smoking. "What do the young people do for work?"

"They don' like working. They all want to go to America or Canada. Or they all waiting for some relative to send money back so they can live it up."

It was a cynical point of view that Rommel never heard expressed from the Guyanese expatriates in Canada. They all extolled the benefits of returning to live in Guyana, from the pleasant climate, to the extent which their Canadian currency stretched.

"Where you going to live?" Ram said.

"I bought a piece of land and built my own house."

"That's nice. Coming back to live off the fat of the land or do business?"

"I'm retired now. Want to do nothing but relax and take it easy."

"And how about your family? They coming too?"

"Eventually."

"You 'ave relatives in Independence Boulevard?"

"My sister is Milady. They call her Lady. Her husband is Earnest but he died in nineteen-ninety-eight. Their son is Mitchell. They all live at 200. Do you know them?"

Ram glanced at him. "Everybody in the Boulevard know Mitchell. But Lady long gone. I think she living in one of the islands now. Might be Trinidad or Barbados, I can't remember."

That was news to Rommel. It had been a couple of months since he'd been in touch with his sister but she'd never told him of a plan to leave Guyana, certainly not in any of her letters to him. He'd been relying on her to smoothe his return and help him integrate back into the society he'd left so many years ago. And what was Ram implying when he said *everyone in the Boulevard knew Mitchell?*

"So, who is living in their old house at 200?"

"Is Mitchell living there. But is not an old house anymore, you know. He rebuild it. Is now the best looking house in the Boulevard."

Was there another reason why everyone knew Mitchell? His sister had told Rommel that her son had a reputation as someone who did everything in a big way. Smoked and drank excessively. Big time Gambler. Women all over the place. Mitchell was a security guard who worked sporadically. So, where did the money come from for him to enjoy his lifestyle? Was he also dealing drugs or involved in crime?

"Tell me what else you know about Mitchell?"

Ram squirmed in the driver's seat and shook his head. "Ah don' like to talk bad about people. What address you build the house?"

"Two-five-two."

Ram shook his head and lapsed into silence.

They came to the Boulevard. Ram made a right and Rommel was counting the house numbers as he passed. They came to an empty lot. Ram stopped the car and pointed in the direction of the lot. Even in the dark, Rommel was able to see, from the light cast by the two adjacent houses, that the property was overgrown with bramble bush and tall paragrass. But no house.

Rommel came out of the car, Ram behind him. They went closer to the lot. A dilappidated paling fence in front lay half-way to the ground. It looked as if it would collapse soon. The gate in the middle of the fence still hung on the top hinge.

"This can't be," Rommel said. "There must be some mistake."

Ram pointed to the house on the right. "That there is number two-fifty. Look at the sign." He pointed to the house on the left. "That there is two-fifty-four. This lot in the middle is two-fifty-two."

"Something's wrong. Lady sent me pictures of the house when it was being constructed and I have one of it completed." Rommel reached into his jacket pocket and pulled out the photograph. He turned it over to Ram who scrutinized it carefully.

"I know all the houses on the Boulevard. None look like that anywhere."

"There's got to be some mistake."

"Boss, is one of two things happen. Your sister Lady gone to the islands with the money. Or Mitchell rebuild the old house with it. Or both. Your guess is as good as mine."

"Take me to Mitchell. He must know what happened to all the money I sent back to his mother to build my house."

Ram took a few steps and paced back and forth. "Ah don' think that's a good idea. That man deal in drugs and the underworld. People who deal with him disappear and never seen again."

"But what am I going to do? All my life savings were sunk into this property."

Ram sighed. He looked at his watch. "You still gat the land and be thankful you still gat your life. We can still make it for the return flight to Canada."

11. HOW I CAME TO BE HERE

[2ND PRIZE NON-FICTION BWG 2020 COMPETITION]

By Mark Blair

TIME: One Late Fall Wednesday Afternoon
EVENT: Memoirs Writing Group Meeting
LOCATION: The Boardroom, Four Corners Library

We are sitting around a large table, in chairs with wheels. Across from me is Rena, politely forthright and in possession of a quick mind. She is not going *gentle into that good night*, of that I am sure. In the far corner is Ursula, full of childlike charm and happy memories.

And then there is Bev, eagerly wanting to make a difference in everyone's life. "That was so wonderful," she said, after James had done reading his story; then searched frantically for the wonderful aspect of it all.

It is the end of the meeting. Mary walks over.

"Mark," she says kindly, holding two sheets of paper close to her chest. "Do you think this is something you feel comfortable doing?"

I assure her I do.

"Perfect," she smiles and neatly places the papers in front of me on the table. "If you would just write your name and email address on this one, here…and here is the schedule of our meetings for you to keep."

I don't have a pen, so she offers hers, setting it down straight on the paper. She waits for me to write, murmurs *perfect* again, takes pen, and paper on which I had written my name, and returns to her seat. I feel like I'm the new kid in kindergarten, like I've just been given a drawing book and brand-new crayons.

Anyway, the room is warm and cozy; but outside, it is *freezing*. Through the window, I see someone wrapped in a black coat disappearing hurriedly in the heavy fog. Looking down, I'm embarrassed to see muddy slush still clinging to the edges of my own soles from having had to walk some way to the building—the curse of travelling by public transportation.

As I had stepped out unto crunching snow into the biting cold at the stop across and up the road, I too had had to wrap myself up tightly, hurrying the lights to change. Still, if anyone cared, they would have seen me smiling to myself while crossing the intersection.

The two babies in the bus, a boy and girl, had seemed as if they had been having their own conversation in that packed mechanical womb. The boy, who had been more interested in quietly staring at everyone, suddenly breaking out into dribbly smiles and saying *Mama,* had so quickly bored the girl that she had turned her attention to the old man sitting nearby. And only heaven knew what she was happily telling him.

They had boarded the bus after it had stopped for the umpteenth time, kneeling then to accommodate the girl in her stroller—a cocoon of layers and layers of cloth secured by straps—and her mother. The stroller had come first, the mouth of the girl inside running at nine knots an hour. The whole bus had lit up at the loud sound of her tiny voice so much that the stoic face of the elderly man sitting up front broke into a wide smile while he was getting up to make way for them. Then he had to move again for they were not the only ones. Another stroller with the boy was being hurriedly, even violently, pushed onto the bus in what had seemed for all intents and purposes, a veritable baby invasion from the cold.

We had then been near Rutherford and Queen, that old inner-city sort of place, after having passed through the industrial West Drive, after the fallen and derelict spirit of Clarke Avenue, after the tree-lined boulevard of City Centre Drive, after leaving the new Bramalea Bus Terminal. Each leg of the journey had its own character like the wrapped and huddling and sniffing figures that continually stopped the bus to embark or disembark: the elderly man, two garrulous gossips, a couple of high schoolers, a lonely fellow, a worried mother. As each came and went, I invented stories about them— where they had come from, where to and why.

The two Mormon missionaries with whom I had been having a pleasant conversation had gotten off at the Terminal. Their obvious sincerity and faith in Mormonism, something very foreign to me, were truly impressive. Kind, eager, nice, attractive, well but modestly dressed, two blond American girls, nineteen years old in Canada, they were walking about seeking potential converts. My promise to attend their meetings had made them obviously happy. And it had made me so too since I always wanted to know what went on behind the closed doors of their imposing temple on Bramalea and Bovaird.

It was interesting to see the way they went about *witnessing.* On boarding the bus, they enthusiastically greeted the driver—Missionaries must always look on the bright side of life, I guess. After engaging him in small talk, they took their seats up front; then glancing in my direction, began urging each other in turn to approach. Eventually, the braver of the two did; the other close behind.

"Good afternoon. And how're you today?"

"It's cold outside," I replied.

"Yeah, I know. But it's so warm in here."

The braver wasted no time: "We're from the Church of Jesus Christ of Latter-day Saints and we were wondering if perhaps you'd be interested in studying the Book of Mormon with us. By the way, I'm Sister Barton—"

"And I am Sister Westerlind," the other quickly interjected, as if self-correcting.

"I'm Mark."

"Pleased to meet you, Mark! As in *Mark* of the Bible? MARK?" Sister Barton said.

"Maybe I was reincarnated."

"Yeah, right." Sister Barton said. "Have you ever read the Book of Mormon, Mark?"

She sat next to me and the other made herself comfortable in the seat before us. After rummaging through her bag for a while, she pulled out a blue book the size of a Harlequin emblazoned with silver letters.

"I can't say that I have, no."

To that, Sister Barton leapt to it. "I'm quoting from Moroni, chapter 10, verse 4," she began. "*And when ye shall receive these things, I would exhort you that ye would ask God, the Eternal Father, in the name of Christ, if these things are not true; and if ye shall ask with a sincere heart, with real intent, having faith in Christ, he will manifest the truth of it unto you, by the power of the Holy Ghost.* Do you think that God would lie to you, Mark?"

Now THAT had been right out of the blue!

I was thankful for their company though. The journey up until then had been pretty lonely and, because of the fog outside, too long as well. Not many people were on the trip, at least not that early on. I had been sitting at the back of the bus by the window, lost in thought the whole time. Only a year ago, I was thinking, I never thought I would have been *being chauffeured* through that particular intersection at precisely that particular time and was wondering where I was going to be at precisely the same time again in a year.

As the bus approached stops to pick up passengers, I was entertaining myself with the view through the window, watching the hooded figures that had been huddling together in the sheds materializing out of the dense fog, hands dug deep in coat pockets, heads hidden in thick fur hoods.

I understood perfectly the longing they must have felt for our arrival. I too had been standing at my own stop praying for the bus to come, which it had done, eventually, after a very long five minutes behind schedule, its red and amber lights squinting through the pervasive fog ahead of its slow and careful approach. On stopping, its doors had swung open with a loud hiss, the speaker inside echoing loudly that the trip was "One, Queen to Mount Pleasant Go Station."

Upon quickly stepping aboard, I had tapped my card, then taken my seat at the back, *extremely* grateful for the warmth, never minding the muddy floor, only hoping I was going to be at the Library in an hour, in time for 2pm.

12.   FATHER, SON AND THE HOLY GHOST
By Michael Joll

On a chilly autumn afternoon, an old man stood by his wife's grave and collected his thoughts.

*

As a boy at his boarding school, he'd devoured the occult paperback novels of Dennis Wheatley, by flashlight, beneath his bed covers.

He was a timid boy of eleven or twelve then and, terrified out of his mind, read the books one after another to overcome his fear of Death. He knew, from no greater an authority than Dennis Wheatley himself, that Death constantly stalked him, always just out of sight, ready to tap his shoulder. If he turned his head swiftly to catch Death unprepared, it was never there, and he relaxed for a moment. When quizzed by the other boys in his dormitory he professed, in a display of bravado that belied the truth, to love the books. "All rubbish," he said in his treble voice. "There are no such things as ghosts."

"Yes, there are," came the several replies in hushed voices—for talking after lights out was an offence punishable by anywhere from a reprimand to six of the best, depending on which prefect caught you.

"It says so in the Bible," offered one hesitant voice.

"And the Father and the Son," added another. "It says so. Somewhere."

"It's bollocks," the Dennis Wheatley fan replied, trying to minimize the quaver in his thin voice.

The voices grew louder and the language coarser as the discussion enveloped all eight boys.

The door opened. "Enough," a deep voice barked. "All of you, the boot shed after breakfast. I'll decide of how many in the morning." The door closed.

A sepulchral silence descended until one voice whispered, "It's your fault, idiot."

*

As a teenager, no longer at boarding school, he had to walk twice daily to his school past the ruins of the Church of the Holy Ghost. Though he no longer read Dennis Wheatley, those stories still haunted and tortured his imagination. For four months of the year, it was twilight or fully night when he passed the darkened ruins. He heard an owl once, breaking cover, and sprinted for home, gasping for breath behind the locked bathroom door.

There were ghosts there, at the Holy Ghost ruins. It made sense. They watched for the unwary, waiting for a dawdler to pass. Or for some foolhardy person to stop and light a cigarette, in defiance of Death. Then Death would wrap you in its arms and spirit you away. Everyone knew that. Only a fool didn't hurry past the graveyard.

He didn't know how old the ruins were. The earliest grave markings, worn all but flat by rain, feet and time, dated from 1348 and the Black Death. Some said the church was destroyed during the Reformation but the graveyard was still in use in the mid-1840s, if you believed the dates on some headstones. Two of the ruined church's stone walls, shedding crumbling mortar like dead skin, stood at an angle in precarious support of the skeletal remains, and a sightless window gaped unblinking. Tall evergreens, among them yews and hemlock—which everyone knew were poisonous—shaded the gravestones peering over the seed heads of the uncut grass. A prickly holly bush brooded in a dark corner marking the rotted stumps where the lych gate used to stand.

All around the young man smelled decay and Death, seeking him to feed its insatiable appetite. He believed.

*

Decades later, when arthritis and the weather permitted, the old man who had once been terrorized by the mention of ghosts strolled through the cemetery in a different town on a different continent. Death, and its constant companions, ghosts, no longer frightened him. His parents, his wife, a son had all stepped over the threshold of the event horizon and been sucked irretrievably into the black hole. So many he had once known and loved had passed through this life that he had come to regard Death as commonplace, as unremarkable as a Tim Hortons coffee.

He couldn't prevent a tear from trickling down his white stubbled cheek; he never could. He wiped the tear away with the back of a chapped hand and swallowed the lump that formed in his throat. He shivered, for it was a cold,

All Saints Day afternoon with dusk falling and the leaves gone from all but a pair of sentinel columnar oaks standing guard over the cemetery gates. He stood alone, yet not completely alone. A presence, unseen, watched him as he touched the pink granite headstone with its simple inscription and his name next to hers, the second date blank. He felt the presence within him and knew from the warmth enveloping him that it came from the only woman he had ever loved.

He still believed.

An image of the Holy Ghost ruins ran through his mind. How silly, he thought, that we trivialize ghosts at Halloween as if they were nothing but small children beneath torn sheets, watched over by parents who should know better. The Trick-or-treaters knew nothing; no more than he did when he was their age. Innocence, perhaps, carried its own blessing.

He thrust his hand in his coat pocket and pulled out a bite-size Mars bar, one he'd saved from the shell-outs the night before. He peeled the wrapper and popped the treat in his mouth. A smile crossed his creased face as he bit in to the chocolate and caramel.

"Not today, my love," he whispered. "But soon."

13.   A PROVINCE OF DEVILS

[2nd PRIZE FICTION BWG 2020 COMPETITION]
By Raymond Holmes

Brent Gardiner couldn't believe what happened. It felt like a trap had been set for him. One moment everything was fine and the next, a disaster.

The words, "you're hired," he heard over the telephone in September, 1976 put him on top of the world. After graduating from university with a master's degree in Electrical Engineering and sending out numerous resumes, he landed a plum sales job with a major industrial instrument company providing an excellent starting salary plus commission.

Brent had never sold before but convinced himself he could. "All goods and services have to be sold," someone once told him. All you had to do was talk to people about what you had to offer—right? Sales careers paid well and he looked forward to the perks associated with the job—a new company car, generous expense account and profit-sharing plan. Other salesmen he encountered didn't seem to work that hard. His skill at selling himself must have been exemplary. Hadn't he convinced the Canadian Sales Manager and that man's boss to hire him even with no sales experience? With such persuasive ability he couldn't fail.

After six weeks training at the U.S. head office in Los Angeles, Brent emerged as a Technical Sales Representative. He had much to learn about their expensive, complicated products and how they were applied. At times he thought his brain would explode from absorbing product specifications and application papers. Being focused on landing the job, Brent didn't think to ask about his sales territory.

"You will have all of Eastern Canada as your sales territory from the middle of Toronto," his boss Bill Harvey, the Canadian Sales Manager said on the first day of his return from the training course.

Brent felt his diaphragm tighten and prickling heat creep up his neck upon hearing the enormous geographic area he was expected to cover. Time to buy a larger suitcase.

Bill continued. "We're counting on you to develop the business in Quebec. That province has been neglected since the last salesperson resigned. They speak French there, but you'll get along okay. Hope you picked up lots of product smarts in California."

Quebec? French? The task of having to sell in that province hadn't occurred to Brent. He smiled and nodded, attempting to project self-assurance, but his intestines felt like they were coiled into a hangman's knot. Having no sales experience and a portfolio of sophisticated products to sell to French-speaking people was like having to cook a seven-course gourmet dinner over a small campfire using a single pot.

As he thought about the situation the noose in his guts tightened. Could he convince customers to purchase complicated technical equipment? How would he manage such a gigantic sales territory and large quota?

Brent had never been to Quebec but knew about the political crisis that occurred in 1970. The malcontents seemed quiet now, but there *was* that issue of French language. Brent's French language skills were limited to the lyrics of a raunchy 1974 song which asked the question: "Voulez vou couche avec moi, ce soir?" He snickered when his friend Mark him the words meant, "Would you like to go to bed with me tonight?" What had he gotten into? Feeling overwhelmed, he didn't sleep well at night.

When Brent opened the newspaper on the morning of November 15, 1976 the headline of apocalyptic gloom hit him like a runaway logging truck.

PARTI QUEBECOIS ELECTED IN QUEBEC. Separatists take over the government in a landslide. The beginning of the end for Canada as we know it.

Stress expanded his anxiety like a child's over-filled balloon about to pop. As a unilingual Anglophone, he would be resented and unwelcome in Quebec. Nobody there would buy what he had to sell or even talk to him. The timing couldn't be worse—a career ruined before it started. The country seemed to be coming apart at the seams. The P.Q. added to the wall of Anglophone worry by stating that their mandate included separating Quebec from the rest of Canada.

Dwelling on the matter, Brent's mind envisioned a province inhabited by antagonistic, hostile people who hated the rest of Canada—a province of devils. He thought of quitting his new job.

His boss, Bill Harvey, a transplanted American, laughed at his concerns.

"The P.Q. agenda will take years to implement and things won't change overnight," he said. "Most of the technical managers and professionals in Quebec are Anglophone or at least English-speaking. They don't manufacture what you're selling in Quebec and have no choice but to buy it from outside the province. There's nothing to worry about."

Brent gave a salesman's reassuring smile, but when a person tells you not to worry, that's exactly what you do.

Bill passed Brent the sales contact books used by the previous salesman who resided in Montreal. Many of the entries bore French names. Brent couldn't read the accompanying notes written in French. They may as well have been in Swahili.

"A few French words will come in handy for you," Bill said. "Remember the phrases *bon jour* and *je ne parle pas Francais*.

Bill explained they meant, "Good day," and "I do not speak French." Brent repeated the phrases but didn't believe that restricted vocabulary would take him far.

"Oh—and you'll see *Est*, *Ouest*, *Nord* and *Sud* on the road signs," Bill added. "Those words mean east, west, north and south. Knowing them will come in handy when you drive in the province."

Brent imagined trying to ask directions with that narrow lexicon and concluded that such counsel from a unilingual Albany, New York expatriate would be of little use.

"Start with our important customers," Bill said. He flipped opened one of the Quebec sales contact books and pointed to an entry. It read: *Gulf Raffinerie, Varennes, Quebec—Philippe St. Armand, Directeur De L'Automatisation.* "You need to make this man your first sales call in Quebec."

"Does he speak English?" asked Brent, in a hopeful tone.

"Of course. He's our key contact at the Gulf Refinery plant. His title means Manager of Plant Automation. We've heard Gulf is planning a major upgrade of one of their processing units. Get all the details on the project and convince him that our products are the best for his needs."

"Will do," said Brent, smiling, pulling at his sticky collar and feeling the onset of indigestion from the greasy lunch curdling his insides. That customer's impressive title was intimidating and the responsibility of selling him on the company's products for a major project, daunting. Reality hit him like a bowling ball falling off a shelf.

After several attempts, Brent reached Mr. St. Armand on the telephone and requested an appointment.

"I can fit you in next Tuesday at nine a.m.," the man said, in an abrupt tone. He spoke with an accent and made no small talk before hanging up. Brent imagined his competitors would also be clamouring for an appointment to discuss the impending facility expansion and the many instruments it would require. They'd be like flies attracted to a pecan pie.

The following Monday Brent embarked upon his first sales trip to Quebec. The journey from Toronto to Montreal was about a ten-hour drive along Highway 401, but three stops to visit customers in Cobourg, Kingston and Cornwall extended the duration. That day in December started well, but at Kingston a raging blizzard began, lasting all the way to Montreal.

A quivering wreck by the time he pulled into the Longueil Holiday Inn parking lot at ten thirty p.m. that evening with a head screaming for pain killers and body ossified with nervous tension, Brent took two aspirin tablets, soaked in a tub of hot water for thirty minutes and then fell into bed.

Wanting to appear competent and knowledgeable, he rose at 5:30 a.m. the next morning to study technical manuals for the products in his presentation. Would he be able to answer all the questions put to him?

Brent repeated the customer's name, trying to make it roll deftly off his tongue. "Philippe St. Armand—Philippe St. Armand." The name had an elegant sound and he imagined it belonging to a tall, debonair French gentleman, but one who might not be receptive or friendly.

As he prepared to leave for the appointment, the telephone rang.

"Get as much information as possible about the upcoming project at Gulf. Make sure you complete the MPA form," his boss Bill Harvey said.

"Of course," Brent replied, feeling a lump form in his throat. He had forgotten to bring one of the Major Project Activity forms designed to manage large project pursuit strategy.

"Good luck," Bill said, with an upbeat voice. "Sell our features and benefits compared to the competition. Knock 'em dead."

Brent knew the names of the competitors but hadn't time to research their products before leaving for the trip. What if Mr. St. Armand asked how his products compared with theirs? He skipped breakfast except for two cups of black coffee.

After a forty-minute drive over icy roads, glancing at a map and making several wrong turns, Brent found the refinery in time for the scheduled appointment and announced himself to the attractive, olive-skinned receptionist with full, inviting lips.

"Mr. St. Armand, please. I have an appointment."

She dialed an extension and said, "Oui" several times between uttering sentences in rapid French. Brent fidgeted, trying not to stare at the ample cleavage visible at the top of her low-cut dress.

"He will be right out monsieur," she said. Brent could feel the weight of judgement in her eyes which seemed to say, "You're in way over your head, Anglo."

"Which way to the washroom please?" he asked, sensing the breakfast coffee distending his bladder.

While washing his hands he splashed water over the front of his trousers. It looked like he'd peed himself. He buttoned up his overcoat to hide the wet splotches and reached into a pocket for his business card wallet. It wasn't there. Did he forget it in the car, or the hotel room?

As he emerged from the men's room, Brent observed a short, swarthy man wearing blue work clothes with a hard hat nestled under his arm speaking to the receptionist. She pointed in Brent's direction and the man looked at him.

Brent began to tremble and his legs felt like boiled cannelloni. Little sleep made his eyes feel like rusty ball-bearings in their sockets. He'd kept an important customer waiting. Not having a business card to give to a client was unforgivable. He looked at his briefcase. Did he remember the sales literature?

The underarms of Brent's shirt felt like damp face cloths. A growling noise drifting up from his stomach and a twinge of light-headedness reminded him he hadn't eaten since noon the previous day. Why did he ever think he could be a salesman?

Get hold of yourself, he said while striding up to the reception desk, his heart beating a military march in his chest. Brent extended his hand to the man and said, "How do you do. I'm Philippe St. Armand."

The receptionist covered her mouth and giggled. A wide smile expanded Philippe St. Armand's face. He grasped Brent's hand, shook it and said, "No—*I* am Philippe St. Armand. You are Mr. Brent Gardiner from Process Instruments Incorporated in Ontario—yes? I have been expecting you."

A bonfire of heat rose up Brent's neck and head. Every nerve in his body quivered. He uttered the simple truth. "I'm sorry, sir. I'm new with the company and nervous. You are my first sales call in Quebec. I'm pleased to meet you. Yes, I am Brent Gardiner from PII."

Philippe laughed. "Well, you needn't worry, Brent. We don't eat children or salespeople here. I am your first call in Quebec? What an honour. Let's have coffee and get acquainted. Would you like a donut?"

Upon hearing the word donut, Brent's mouth watered and his stomach sang in low key.

Following that awkward icebreaker and the consumption of two donuts, Brent and Philippe St. Armand got along well. Brent took copious notes concerning the project, explained the features and benefits associated with his company's products and answered all the questions posed to him except one which he promised to follow up with, and did later that day. To his relief, Philippe did not ask how his company's products compared with those of the competition.

Brent made three more calls on Philippe St. Armand, each time remembering the cardinal rule for every salesperson—to close the sale, always ask for the order.

At lunch, on the day of the third call, Philippe shook his hand and said, "The order is yours."

Brent's confidence and self-image soared like a Victoria Day aerial rocket and the proudest day of his life occurred when his bosses' boss, the North American Sales Manager in California called him and said, "Well done in booking that order for Gulf. I'm glad we hired you."

Brent's sales career in Quebec turned out to be successful. He discovered that the province wasn't inhabited by devils after all but populated by ordinary people getting by day-to-day like everyone else. Language didn't change human nature.

14.   TRAVELLING THROUGH THE ALPHABET

By Rena Flannigan

She sits by the window and watches the traffic

Her mind starts to wander over days from her past

She thinks of the places she still wants to see, knowing she won't

Then her mind turns again to the many she did see—some unexpectedly

It would be easy to work through the alphabet listing them all

Sun drenched shores, golden vistas in Indian summer

Black sands of volcanoes, some still erupting

Making some islands bigger, for instance, Hawaii

The aroma of flowers made into leis for visitors

As one island grows bigger, another gets smaller

Prince Edward Island's red earth with its shoreline eroding

Where people eat the best potatoes that ever did grow

Australia's great Outback with mounds made by termites

The wallabies, crocodiles, giant spiders and snakes

Don't mess with them Mate or they might kill you!

Their venom is fatal—it could bring your demise.

The majestic whales swimming in the Pacific

Will glide to Alaska where the water is frigid

Watching them is amazing, their size—tremendous

Their babies might be born in Mexico's warm Banderas Bay

Where sunsets are phenomenal with colours unreal

Nature is marvellous, with shades unbelievable

The glow oe'r the mountains changing minute by minute

The world is a great place to be in, give thanks that you are there

In Athens the political atmosphere due to elections

No less than chaotic, crowds and noise everywhere

Good to see people being so active though it's a bit frightening

A friend says "better not to be here, let's go to our hotel"

Memories come back of lessons learned

Of sculptures and Greek Gods of mythology

Temples, amphitheatres, uneven marble steps to climb

To reach the Parthenon makes it all quite a challenge.

Pink sands in Bermuda and kite flying contests

Amazing how tiny hand-made kites can be

Match box sizes to great big behemoths

Like an artist's palette of colours they fly by

The ancient city of Dubrovnik, so historical to explore

The landscape looks barren, covered in limestone

Hiding rivers from sight in underground caverns

Then came a terrible Civil War

In the third century, a wall built by the Romans

Is a great place to experience, wishing walls could talk

How heartbreaking to see the carnage by fighting

The church, the damaged buildings, the ancient fountain

A lot of wandering from sea to sea

Even walking on a desert where no desert is expected

This is only a small part of her travel alphabet

There is much more to tell but now she is tiring

The years passing by with memories still coming

The old lady sighs as she thinks and recalls them

Knowing how blessed she was to have such good fortune

Seeing so many places and reliving it all as if it was yesterday.

To relate of her travels in Ireland and England

Back to the moors of Scotland and lochs all aglow

To see the heather covering the hillsides

With September vistas of purple, pink and white

Could these be the September of her years?

15.   TARA'S MUSINGS

By Cherry Narula

Tara jumped out of bed as the shrill sound of the alarm pierced through the 6:00 am silence.

Everything was laid out as usual to work like clockwork. She always prepared the night before to be on time to catch a 7:30 am train for work. Getting ready swiftly, Monday to Friday, for the past ten years had become an act of automation and she could go through all the morning routine steps with her eyes closed. Clothes ready to wear hung close to the alarm and the kettle in the kitchen was already pre-set for her morning cup of tea. A banana and a muffin to carry along for the morning coffee break were kept on the kitchen counter. Lunch was packed and ready in the refrigerator.

The train station was a short fifteen-minute walk away. Tara usually aimed to reach there by 7:20 am. Being the originating station, she got her favourite window seat without fail for the hour-long ride to work.

The rhythmic sound of the train soothed Tara as she gazed out the window. The forecast promised a bright and sunny day and overhead, clear white clouds glistened with the rays of the sun. She looked around her—as usual all heads were bent checking their phones. Opening her bag, she pulled out a journal titled *Urban Musings* she had started writing two years ago with a secret dream of publishing it someday. Most of Tara's musings originated either during the train ride, or at the end of the day and during these moments of introspection, her thoughts fed her urge to write. She opened her journal, picked up her pen and tried to keep pace as her thoughts raced. She wrote:

"It's been a while,

I've seen a smile,

That hurried walk,

While fingers tap the talk,

A typed 'Good Morning,'

Even while frowning,

Rushing from point A to B, B to C,

There is so much more than what we see.

The material race is just an illusion,

Free yourself from all delusions,

Understand the real purpose to see,

What a beautiful place this world can be."

Tara glanced around her again. Most heads were still bowed, browsing their phones. Some had their laptops open, making the best use of time to prepare for the workday ahead.

She was looking forward to the day ahead. She loved her job as a design architect and had an incredible team of co-workers—most of them had been working together for five or more years. She firmly believed that working in a team brought out the best in people, and she herself got along splendidly with everyone. Yes, it was true there were days when people would snap at each other since the complexity of their projects led to inevitable tension and conflict. They had just completed a challenging, stressful project and after lunch, they would be having a training session on how to cope with pressure.

Tara pondered and started writing in her journal again. Once again words poured out:

"An important course to attend,

Titled Stress Management.

A very easy way out,

I am so stressed I can always shout.

I simply don't get it,

Somethings just don't fit.

I manage what I keep,

Stress I manage and go to sleep.

What is this quality of sleep and health,

Manage more stress, gather more wealth.

Make the right choice, end the strife,

Stay stress free, live a meaningful life."

It was almost 8:30 am. Tara put her journal away. The train was approaching her station. Her office was at a fifteen-minute walking distance and this was the last station. Everyone got off and briskly walked away but she always enjoyed a leisurely stroll since she had ample time.

The morning flew by swiftly. Half the day was spent brainstorming a new project her team had been assigned. After lunch, everyone got together in the conference room for the Stress Management training. It was indeed a stress buster to attend such a training. Lately, there had been situations that had resulted in conflict. These had brought about disharmony among an otherwise upbeat workforce. In the training session, team members shared their disagreements and confrontations. A lot could be attributed to the type of projects they had recently handled. Some of their recent contracts had several challenges in the designs and construction stages and it had been extremely demanding to meet the deadlines.

During the session, several interactive exercises were done with a goal to train the conscious mind to breeze through complex situations. Various activities to inculcate positive thinking and behaviour to stay healthy were explored and the importance of positive messaging leading to a happier work culture discussed.

Before they knew it, the workday was over—it was 5 pm. Tara headed to the train station, walking briskly this time. Her train would be leaving in twenty minutes. She frequently dozed off on the way back home and found the short nap refreshing. Though an avid reader, she had never been able to get into the habit of reading on the train. When not taking a nap, she preferred to observe and write.

She usually reached home by 6:35 pm. After a shower, she prepared her dinner. All evening chores and preparation for the next day were done by 8pm. That is when she sat back and relaxed.

Her phone rang, it was her mother. She had promised her mother that she would visit her the coming weekend. Her mother and grandmother lived together an hour away. Tara's heart always warmed up when she thought of her ninety-year-old grandmother and she was really looking forward to the weekend visit.

After the call was over, she kept gazing at the darkened summer night sky—some light hues still visible. It was a clear night and Tara could see the full moon accompanied by two bright stars. Filled with an overwhelming surge of contentment, she picked up her journal. She speedily wrote the verse playing in her mind:

> "Innumerable blessing surround,
>
> I went searching and finally found,
>
> All the answers tucked within.
>
> Tireless travels in search of a dream,
>
> Returning exhausted, saw the light beam,
>
> The dream had been a reality all along."

Happy and content, Tara looked around to ensure all was ready for the next morning. She resisted the temptation to turn on the television and instead read a book. At 10 pm, she put her book away to call it a night.

She went to bed to wake up refreshed for her 6 am alarm the next morning. Another day of possibilities, closer to her dream of getting published, adding a few more verses to *Urban Musings*.

16.   THE UNDERGROUND
By Ken Puddicombe

"How did you manage to get released?" Tom said.

"It wasn't easy," Beverley said. "Son of a bitch Wong put me through the ringer, wanted to know where the latest underground tunnel was located, and for me to name names."

"What did you tell him?"

"Nothing. The new Aromaless cigarettes help. They can't detect smokers easily these days."

"Won't be long before they come up with something to counter it, though. Must have been a real battle of wills between you and Wong."

"It was. How did *you* escape? I thought for sure they had you cornered."

"I gave them the slip and went down a back alley."

The tunnel was packed all the way to the rear, much more so tonight than Beverley had ever seen on previous occasions.

Even though she and Tom had arrived late it wasn't long before they were pushed and compressed further into the dark, dank underground sewer, one of hundreds sanctioned by the committee. The sewer system had quickly become the last resort for those who were determined not to surrender to the smoking ban, and the stench had proved effective, allowing them to avoid detection, so far.

Beverley shivered. The only comfort against the biting cold came from the cigarette they were sharing, that and the heat generated by the other bodies. There were many groups sharing, people passing a cigarette from one to the other. Based on the size of the tunnel, she figured that there had to be at least a thousand people. With more than fifty much larger venues still undetected, she thought that the movement was still on the increase, despite all efforts by the government to track and eliminate them.

Beverley took another drag on the cigarette. "This is good shit," she said. "Where did you get it?"

Tom shrugged and took the cigarette. He inhaled deeply and the glow from the cigarette lit up his face enough for her to see the amount of pleasure he was experiencing. He looked like a kid locked in a pastry shop, someone who can't believe his good fortune would last forever, and so he has to make the most of it.

It was more than a minute before Tom exhaled and responded.

"Same as all the others," he said. "Bought it on the black market."

Cigarettes had been taxed heavily back in the 2020 budget when the government was desperately looking to fund the growing demand on the health services. Governments had always raised a significant portion of their revenue through *Sin Taxes*, but this time the levies became so onerous that several companies went out of business. Ten years later, those that remained were successfully sued by governments and many had to declare bankruptcy, unable to pay the billions in fines imposed by the courts. It took another five years for the anti-smoking lobby to convince the government that additional legislation was needed, and smoking had been completely banned. The few manufacturers who refused to quit went underground.

Beverley leaned closer to Tom to get a whiff of the smoke he was exhaling. In the glow of a thousand cigarettes, there was a distinct blue haze overtaking the entire tunnel. The latest trend was the mixing of tobacco with marijuana and this had been well received by those who were against the ban.

At times, Beverley couldn't figure who was the more addicted between her and Tom. She'd come from a family of non-smokers but had picked up the habit more so to rebel against the growing interdiction than from the fulfillment of a craving. Tom had started even before he turned ten. He'd come from a family of smokers and it had been a real challenge for him, especially after they passed the law outlawing the tobacco companies and smoking became a prohibited act, punishable by a fine for the first infraction, rehabilitation for the second, jail for subsequent offences.

It had been three days ago when the underground they were in, an abandoned tunnel that had been constructed to connect Centre Island to Toronto was raided by CSASS—the Canadian Squad Against Smoking and Smokers. Beverley and Tom had made their way to the back of the tunnel and escaped by climbing a ladder leading up to a manhole. In the early days of the movement, hundreds of people were picked up easily and it was only after emergency exits were added to every tunnel that flight from the CSASS became possible. But, on this occasion, just as they emerged through the manhole cover, they found the squad waiting for them. She was certain that someone had squealed, not only about the location, but about the emergency exits also. In addition to having to worry about people in the movement squealing to gain favours, they also had to be on guard for vigilantes—armed squads of roving citizens on the lookout for smokers. There were reports circulating about a few smokers being shot on sight.

"You were lucky," Beverley said.

"I know. It's getting tougher and tougher to evade them with that heat and smoke equipment they're using these days."

The technology had changed radically over the last decade, some of it for better. Sure, diabetes had been virtually eradicated with the introduction of engineered pancreas. Body parts could be bought off the shelf: there were manufactured kidneys, livers, pancreas, all coded with the recipient's genetic code for implantation. Cancer had decreased by over eighty percent. AIDS and the common cold had been eradicated with the discovery of new antiviral drugs. These were all things that had helped to raise the life span to nearly one hundred and twenty-five years. And people never looked and felt better. Baldness drugs were now available for both men and women. Artificial skin transplants meant a society free of wrinkles. People never suffered the discomfort or embarrassment of dentures—teeth were replaced by implants. But, with the improvement in health had come growing government intrusion in the lives of its citizens, something the underground movement was formed to combat.

"You can still outrun the best of them," Beverley said, with a certain amount of admiration.

Tom shook his head. "There's coming a day, though, when I won't be able to get away from them."

Tom had always been able to outrun SAS. He was one of the Bionic athletes, people who had artificial knees, ligaments and muscles. Olympic rules had been relaxed to accommodate them since many athletes worldwide had found ways to utilize the technology. It was at the 2024 Olympics in Cape Town, the first in Africa, that she'd met Tom and they'd started living together a short while after.

Beverley shook her head. It was the uncertainty that got to her most of all; they never knew where it would end. It was like pulling a loose string from a quilt and having no idea about the actual length of the thread.

"I'm so tired," she said. "I feel like I could sleep for a year. Why can't they just leave us alone to carry on with our lives?'

She hadn't been allowed to sleep for two days and nights during Wong's interrogation…

He'd come into the interrogation room time and again. Just as she was about to nod off, he'd return and wake her with more questions.

"Tell me where the next Smokevention is and I'll let you go," Wong said.

He carried around his short, rotund body with an agility that defied his size, bobbing around the room in his uniform and constantly stopping directly in front of her to blow smoke in her face. The irony of what he was doing could hardly escape her. Here was the man in charge of eradicating the institution of smoking in Canada, and yet he was using the very act to torture her.

"You know we're going to get all of you, sooner or later," Wong said. "Why don't you make it easy on yourself and tell me what I want to know. I can make it worthwhile for you."

She was intrigued. "How are you going to do that?"

Another puff of smoke in her face, followed by: "Unlimited cigarettes in payment. You'd never have to worry again about satisfying your craving. Or, we could put you through the program, if you want."

The *program*—she'd heard enough of that to know it was the last thing she wanted. Those who participated were pumped full of drugs containing a cocktail of Nicontrolic, Nicofin and Nicotitrelief. It either killed you or cured you but the government had refused to release information and Statistics Canada had been so emasculated as an institution that there was no data available. If CSASS had any doubt the cure had worked, you were shackled with an electronic monitor that tracked your movements and filtered the air around you, sending back messages to CSASS.

"You have nothing on me," she said. "You have to let me go."

Wong sat down across the table and accessed an electronic tablet he'd been toting around. He had a way of parting his lips and opening his mouth wide, and when he did, his even, white teeth were on display. He was obviously not a habitual smoker. He was someone who only took pleasure in it to show he had the power to do it. Here was a man, she thought, who would actually like going to the dentist, someone who liked the feel of the drill, the shaking, rattling, whirring, buzzing that creates a sensation he would actually get high on. "Give me more," would be his thought as he sat in the chair.

"Why are you giving me a hard time? I can take good care of you, if you let me. We have a lot in common, you and me," Wong said, as he scrolled down the tablet.

"I doubt that very much."

Wong continued, as if he hadn't heard her. "We're both cut from the same cloth, so to speak."

"What do you mean?"

"I see that your great-grandparents came from Guyana, in South America."

"So?"

"Mine did too, around the same time, back in the nineteen sixties. They were all coming here to give their children a better life. It's what we're trying to do here, now. Why don't you help us?"

Beverley laughed. "That's funny. I heard that they left the old country because of a brutal dictatorship, and now we seem to be going down the same road here."

Wong ignored the remark and looked at his tablet. "Says here that you applied for a child permit twice and you were rejected because you didn't pass the means test."

He had to be accessing the government's central database. What other information did they have on her? It was rumored that they knew everything about you these days, right down to your smoking habits. Wong would also know that Tom had been a sperm donor before he was sterilized in his early teens. His sperm was now held in a central bank, monitored and doled out by authorities, to be used in artificial placenta and vitro fertilization, a process regulating childbirth from conception right down to delivery.

Beverley sniggered. *Means Test*: it was an oxymoron for a process to determine whether you were fit to be a parent. The Department of Conception developed a dossier of the applicant, no doubt with information from the central database. Based on a number of different factors ranging from your ability to provide for the child to your psychological profile, you were deemed eligible for parenthood or rejected outright, with no explanation provided. The Freedom of Information Act had been abolished long ago and no one could access government information, but Beverley was sure that smoking would have played a major part in the decision.

"I can fix things so that you have a permit," Wong said.

Beverley shook her head. "No deal. It's a bit too late for that. Either book me, or let me go."

*

Beverley stirred. She'd been sleeping on Tom's shoulder. The tunnel had grown even more crowded and the noise level had increased substantially. A few people had fallen into the sewer and climbed back out with the help of others in the group. Tom was still smoking. She'd thought it was the only one he'd had and was surprised to see another cigarette between his lips. He seemed to have a secret stash that he was not sharing with her, something unlike him.

Sooner or later they had to leave and go out again, hoping to escape detection. It was growing much more difficult in the city than the rural areas facing a prolonged dry spell. Forest fires had already wiped out thousands of acres of prime forest. The government was unable to detect smokers there, as much as they were unable to control the fires raging out of control.

The tunnels in the city had become the last escape for smokers, and all around she saw nervous people coming to the end of their community cigarette. Tom was no different—he looked like a bird that had grown accustomed to the security of its cage and was fearful that if he left he might meet some unknown peril and not know how to deal with it.

A sudden calm rippled through the entire tunnel. It was like being in the eye of a hurricane.

Everyone stopped and listened.

"Do you hear that?" Beverley said.

Tom shook his head. "Don't hear anything."

"Yes, it's coming from the direction of the entrance."

It was where everyone's attention was focused.

"You're imagining things," he said. "There's nothing back there."

But people had already started to head for the escape tunnel in the rear.

"We should go," she said.

"There's nothing to be afraid of," Tom said. "Wait here with me. I will take good care of you."

Wong had said the same thing, that he would take good care of her.

She ran with the others. The last time she looked back, Tom was calmly puffing away on his cigarette, looking as if he didn't have a care in the world.

17.   THE C-WORD

By Michael Joll

When you have it, it occupies top of mind. You can't ignore it, hoping it will go away like a zit or a touch of rheumatism. But, on the positive side, when you have cancer you get to meet some of the nicest, kindest people in the world.

It's September 2014. A warm afternoon. A beer on the deck. Maybe two. It leads to a trip indoors. It's supposed to be a beer colour, not Merlot. It's not my imagination. I'm in the doctor's office in an hour, so I know it must be serious when they can fit me in so quickly.

"It could be many things," the doctor said, reaching for the Readers Digest Compendium of Medical Symptoms on the shelf above his desk. "Have you been eating beetroot?"

"No."

"Hmm." He checked my tongue and throat, presumably for tonsils. "Hmm," he mused again. I didn't think that an absence of tonsils could lead to red pee, but you never know. It's all connected.

"I think we'll do an ultrasound. And I'm referring you to a urologist. Just to be on the safe side. And a nephrologist." I had to look up nephrologist when I got home. "Any trouble with the prostate?" I shook my head. "Could be a UTI," he said, not sounding over positive in his initial diagnosis. "It could be a bladder tumour," he mumbled, probably hoping I'd miss it. He didn't mention the C-Word.

I'd already looked up the symptoms on *Mayo.com* and *Wikipedia.* I could have saved him the trouble.

"Drink a litre of water an hour before the ultrasound," the receptionist at the ultrasound office told me when I booked the appointment. Water? A litre? Beer, maybe, but water? "Water," she emphasized. "No additives." A week away. A week to fret about how I was going to keep a litre of water inside me for an hour without an incident.

When I got to see the urologist, he was courteous and professional. Abrupt is another word that springs to mind. "The hospital will call you. I'm going to do a cystoscopy. Sign here." He thrust a sheet of paper covered with an indecipherable, left-handed scribble in front of me. It looked like Arabic to me. I signed away my life, probably my house as well, and first dibs on my next grandchild.

Armed with the paperwork I went home and looked up cystoscopy on the Internet. I spoke to my brother. He had had several. "It's like having barbed wire shoved up the urethra and pulled out again," he said, not sounding cheerful. "Good luck!"

On the appointed day I lay on the padded operating table. A pleasant young nurse told me to hike up my hospital gown to my waist. She became the first of countless women to take a professional interest in an unmentionable but unremarkable appendage. "I'm going to rub some of this on the tip," she told me, holding up an industrial-size tube with indecipherable lettering on it, rather like the urologist's. "It's a topical anesthetic. It will deaden you a bit. Not much, I'm afraid," she added with a look of 'rather you than me' on her face. "But every little helps, you'll see."

She was as good as her word, applying a liberal dose of gel to the important bit. It worked. Not that anything down there needed deadening. I didn't feel a thing. I didn't even smile. Honest.

The urologist shimmered silently into the operating room, swathed in pale blue from hair net to booties. The nurse inserted a semi-rigid tube the diameter of a fire hose up you know where. Then the urologist shoved a camera the size of an old-fashioned Polaroid on the end of a length of rope the diameter of a transatlantic ocean liner's mooring cable up the tube. I got to watch it on the TV monitor.

"See?" the urologist said with a triumphant note of "Eureka!" in his voice, bringing into focus what I assumed was the bladder wall. I was expecting a drum roll and a crash of cymbals. Didn't happen. "See how the wall is red." He did something to the wire and the camera twisted around for me to get a better look.

"A tumour on the bladder wall." He sounded pleased.

"Not good?" I suggested.

"They're never good." His normally glum voice returned. "I need to take a couple of pictures. How does this camera work?"

I didn't think he was asking me. The nurse showed him.

"Here," he said after reversing the inbound procedure. "See?"

He showed me a couple of photos. An object half the size of a city block and looking rather like a Triffid with tentacles sprouting from one end winked and waved at me. The other end seemed firmly attached to what I took to be the bladder wall. And lo! There was even a red patch, exactly as promised.

"I can operate next week," he said.

"So soon?"

"I had a cancellation." I didn't dare ask after the health of the cancellation. "Sign here, here and here. Consent. See my receptionist this afternoon. She'll give you details. Next!"

*

The sun had yet to rise over Newfoundland when my wife, our older daughter and I arrived at the hospital at the appointed hour. She and said daughter immediately decamped to the coffee shop for java. By that time I had been off solids and liquids for twelve hours. I was ready to kill. They returned, clutching coffee. I spared their lives while they sipped and smirked. Too many witnesses, but a hospital is as good a place as any to dispose of a body.

A pleasant young woman volunteer introduced herself to the three of us. Then she turned her attention to me. "We're going to go and get undressed," she informed me, holding out an encouraging hand. I thought my luck had changed for the better.

"We?"

She had the decency to blush.

At various intervals, more women came to see me, measure me, weigh me, take my vitals, inspect me for signs of physical and mental defects and asked me countless more questions about missing or replaced body parts. I was told to pull on a pair of white surgical stockings. "To prevent blood clots," they said. Great. Just when, on the urologist's orders, I've been off the blood thinners for five days. I looked at my pathetic pale shins before I pulled up the stockings. I knew I should have shaved my legs before leaving the house.

"You'll get a shot of Mighty Mice directly into the bladder, post-op," a nurse barked at me before I left for pre-op.

"Mighty Mice?"

"Mitomycin. Chemo," she growled. "Next!"

Chemo. Great. Now my hair will fall out.

Student nurses hovered around me in pre-op. After they inspected closely the externals of the afflicted area, we shared laughs at my discomfort. Even the anesthesiologist, a sub-sept of the medical clan not known for knee-slapping levity, cracked a joke or two at my expense. Perhaps he was Irish. Or from Newfoundland. I could never tell the difference. It was like I was at the pub with old friends. I could have used a pint right about then.

The urologist quizzed me after inspecting my wrist band in case I was an imposter. As if anyone would willingly and knowingly take my place. "Do you know why you're here?" I was rather hoping he knew why I was lying half-naked on an operating table, legs splayed and surrounded by nurses, tubes and beeping machines.

"Um. A transsexual something or other," I said, trying to remember the medical term for the procedure I was expecting to undergo. "You're going to remove a tumour from my bladder." I hoped that was what he also had in mind.

"A trans-urethral resection of a bladder tumour," he said. "TURBT. Quite right."

"It's comforting to know we're both on the same page," I suggested.

The anesthesiologist shoved a needle the size of Nelson's Column into my spine. "Can you feel your toes?"

"Yes."

"Can you raise your legs?"

I obliged.

"How about now?"

"Not so good."

"Now?"

"Uh-uh."

"Good."

Good? How can paralysis from the waist down be good? I played along. "Now make with the happy juice," I said, "while I count backwards from 100." I didn't reach 99.

The nurses in recovery made me comfortable, even though I couldn't feel a thing. They inspected me closely and admired the bandaging that their operating room colleagues had performed on my appendage. From the end of the bandage, tubing hung. This did not portend well.

"The catheter is to drain you," a nurse told me helpfully. I couldn't think of any other use for it, other than using the tubing for a slingshot. Another bevy of nurses arrived to inspect the bandaged handiwork. They rolled me onto my side. "Stay there," they told me, as if I had an option, still fully numb from the waist down. "We'll be back in half an hour to roll you over so the chemo can do its work all over."

An hour later, the night shift came on and we repeated the process of barrel rolling so that the new group of student nurses could receive instruction on how to slosh the chemo around inside me like water in a Swish barrel.

"Come and see me in two weeks for the results," the urologist told me before signing my discharge the morning after the op. "Call my office for an appointment. Sign here." I obeyed. He vanished the same way he'd appeared; like a mirage.

I went home. I checked my discharge papers for helpful post-op hints and further instructions. The papers informed me that I had undergone a TURP—the removal of my prostate. No mention of a bladder tumour. I checked with the urologist's office. "No," the receptionist said. "It was definitely a bladder tumour removal. You must have received the wrong papers. Never mind. It's all the same post-op."

The Friday afternoon before my scheduled Monday morning date with the urologist at his office he phoned me at home. "It's malignant," he said. No, "Hi, how are you," or anything. "It's into the bladder wall. I need to go in again and scrape the tissue clean. Tuesday next week. See my receptionist. You'll have to sign some papers."

"A bit like a D&C?" I suggested.

"Only one bit gets dilated, like before," he said. "Then we scrape the wall."

"With a scalpel?" I imagined a scalpel going up where only liquid should come down.

"We use electrosurgery. To cauterize as we go."

"Hmm," I mused. "Barbequed bladder." But the phone had gone dead. If O.H.I.P. paid by the word, they had a bargain.

A woman came to see me and removed the catheter on the Sunday morning after the operation. There are few experiences in life to match that of freedom from the catheter. My joy proved short-lived. By Tuesday I was shivering uncontrollably. By Wednesday I was worse. I took myself off to bed. "We need to get you to the hospital," my wife told me.

"It will go away eventually," I said, soaked in sweat and freezing beneath the duvet. At eleven that night, I quit. "We're going to the hospital," I said as my wife climbed into her night attire. I threw a parka over my pyjamas for the November chill and pulled on a pair of runners. In the hospital waiting room, a police officer eyed me suspiciously as if I was a Code White escapee from the psych ward. With my violent shaking, I gave a reasonable impression of a drunk with delirium tremens. I'm sure the cop was itching to arrest me.

After the technicians had examined the content of the fluids they'd extracted from me, I saw the doctor. The police officer lurked outside the half-drawn curtain. "What you have, my friend," the doctor said, slapping my back, "is a kidney infection. Sign here, get your wife to fill this prescription in the morning, and sign here and here. Next!"

*

On Tuesday, exactly as the urologist prophesied, we repeated every step of the procedure. The following Friday afternoon, Sandy, my nurse from North Wales for the sessions of follow-up therapy, performed her shtick with lubricating Xylocaine jelly. Then she rammed a rod inside me down which she injected the BCG tuberculosis vaccine directly into my bladder. "It works in about two-thirds of the cases," she told me.

"The other third gets tuberculosis?"

"No," she reassured me. "Not that many."

I noticed Sandy's hands as she removed the rod. "You're married?" I said.

"Thirty years."

"Does your husband know what you do for a living all day?"

"I spare him the details. Turn over."

I turned every fifteen minutes to swish the vaccine around inside me. Like Pepto Bismol, coating. My first session with Sandy drew to a close. I saw her at the nurse's station on my way out.

"That damn BCG vaccine makes me want to pee," I said.

"Too bad. You have another hour to wait before you can oblige it."

"Rats! Are you on next week, Sandy?"

"If you're planning to come back."

"For sure."

"Then I'll be here."

"You're the best, Sandy."

"I won't tell your wife you said that."

"It's all in the wrist," one nurse says as I pass by. They all laugh. They laugh a lot. I figure they must love their work. And they have a lot to laugh about.

Heck, they've seen me without my pants on.

"You will have to use a condom for the next six weeks," was Sandy's parting shot. "You can't be too careful. And no sex for forty-eight hours. You probably won't want to, anyway." I'm nearly seventy. Sounds like a reprieve.

My daughters had already told me about latex use. "For sure," said the younger one. "It's on Wikipedia. I've looked it up already."

"You know what BCG stands for, dad?" The older daughter didn't give me time to say Bacillus Calmette-Guérin before interrupting. "It's for Be Careful, Grandad."

"Yeah, you can't be too careful, Grandad," echoed her sister. "Mom doesn't want TB."

I got to see Sandy and her crew on Fridays for a couple of years: six weeks on, three months off, rinse and repeat. Or maybe it's three weeks on and six months off. It's undignified, but considering the alternative…

When it comes to cancer, attitude is everything. A cure would be good, too. Because of cancer, I met some of the nicest, kindest and funniest people on the planet, but I hope never to see them again, professionally.

Six years post-op and still upright, at my latest, now annual, cystoscopy, they told me cheerfully that I had the best bladder they'd seen all day. I checked the clock on the way out. It was still only 8:30 in the morning. I hoped the others would be as lucky.

18.   ESCAPE TO NOWHERE

By Raymond Holmes

Amira is my name. I am fourteen years old now and was born in a village in Syria near the city of Homs. In Arabic my name means princess, but I do not feel like a royal person. I am of less value than a dog because of what has happened to me and my family.

On my way home from school one afternoon, I heard the thunder of big guns far away from our village. Each day the sounds grew louder until we could see their flashes in the night. Soon the explosions came near and the lights went out at school. My brother Hassan and I were frightened and couldn't concentrate to do our lessons. Father said it was the war, but not to worry since the people fighting had no reason to harm us.

Three days later blasts shook the ground around our house. Mother screamed. The noise hurt my ears. Pictures and dishes fell from the walls and broke. We smelled smoke, heard loud voices and saw people running in the street. Father returned home in distress. His shop had been damaged by the explosions.

The next day soldiers invaded our neighbourhood and came to our house; angry, fierce-looking men carrying guns.

"What do you want with us?" Father said to them. They beat him. Mother screamed for them not to hurt him, but they did not listen to her. His face and head were covered with blood. Hasan and I cried when we saw what they did.

"You protested against the government, didn't you?" they shouted at him over and over.

Father didn't answer them.

"Christian pig," one soldier said and spit on him.

They dragged Father away. That was the last time I saw him.

The way the men looked at Mother and I made me afraid. A soldier touched my hair and asked Mother how old I was.

"She's only eleven and the boy is nine," she said with a look of fear on her face.

I didn't know why Mother lied about our ages but said nothing. Three of the men took her into the other room. We heard struggling and cloth being ripped. She screamed.

"I'll do anything you want," she cried. "Just don't hurt the children."

My body shook with fright. Hassan called out to Mother. A soldier struck him, pushed him against the wall and said to be quiet.

We could hear the low, whimpering voice of our mother. After what seemed like a long time, the men came out fastening their clothes and laughing.

They took everything of value from our house, upset furniture, emptied drawers and broke dishes.

After they left, we went in to see Mother. She was sitting on the edge of the bed sobbing, her torn clothing clutched to her body, face red and wet with tears. She pulled us close.

"I'm all right," she said. "If we wait and are quiet, the men will go and peace will come."

Calm did not come to the village. The sound of gunfire, explosions and screaming kept us awake all night.

For two days Mother searched for our Father and other family members while we stayed with a neighbor named Yusuf and his family. They were Muslims, but he was our father's best friend from when they were children.

The sound of guns and bombs continued. We were afraid for our Mother when she left the house each day and begged her not to go, but she returned safely.

She said our grandparents' and uncles' houses were damaged and empty. There was no sign of them, or Father.

A day later our world fell apart when a neighbor told us Father had been killed together with other men in the main square.

Mother fell to her knees in the doorway. "Dear God. What will become of us now," she wailed.

Hassan and I cried for a long time. I couldn't believe we would never see our Father again. What would we do without him? I was so afraid I could hardly breathe and tasted the bitter flavour of fear in my mouth.

"You must leave the village," Yusuf said to Mother. "Many of your friends and neighbours have already done so. Christian people are being killed."

"I will not leave our home," she said. "I must locate my family and bury the body of my husband."

"No. You must go now," Yusuf said. "Your husband is beyond suffering and there is no time to search for the others. They are killing all the non-Muslims and they will come back for you and your children. I beg you to leave this place."

Mother's face whitened and her eyes filled with terror. We wrapped our arms around her and started to cry. I could feel her body trembling. Panic filled me and I thought we might be killed at any moment. Had God forsaken us?

"How can we leave and where will we go?" Mother said.

"I will help you get away," Yusuf told her. "It is my duty before Allah to assist the family of my best friend. There are refugee camps in Lebanon near the Syrian border. You will be safe there. It is a dangerous journey, but I beg you to go there while you still can."

I wanted to stay in the house and hide.

We left that evening. A bright moon hung in the sky like a silver brooch surrounded by stars sparkling like diamonds. Mother bought bread, cheese and bottles of water to take with us using money she had concealed in the wall of our house before the soldiers came.

Yusuf hid near a ruined building down the street watching the road for soldiers. We crouched behind the remains of a burned car, waiting. A blackened, faceless body sat upright in the driver's seat, its charred hands gripping the steering wheel like claws and mouth gaping in a solidified moment of agony. Sickness rose in my throat at the sight of it. Finally Yusuf waved to us that the way was clear.

"We can go now, but be very quiet," Mother whispered. Her eyes were wide, face tight and pale. She squeezed my hand so hard it hurt. I could smell the perfume of her fear.

The guns and bombs had destroyed everything familiar in our neighborhood. We treaded carefully around piles of wreckage, watching and listening for soldiers. Broken glass crackled under my feet and I stumbled over wooden beams and bricks.

We moved between ruined buildings and came upon the bodies of men, women, and children scattered in a street.

I had never seen so many dead people before and froze at the sight, my feet rooted in the ground. Their mouths hung open and faces twisted. Dismembered arms and legs torn from bodies lay close by. I vomited when I recognized a girl from my school with belly torn open and insides spilled out like rope. Hassan clung to my dress and started to cry. Mother clamped a hand over his mouth and pulled us away. The night air chilled me, and any moment I expected bullets to rip through my body.

With Yusuf guiding us, we walked all night and most of the next day, stopping to hide at hearing any sound. Guns roared behind us in the distance. Exhausted and frightened, I caught only brief periods of sleep. Hassan and I wanted to lie down and rest more, but Mother wouldn't let us.

"If you lay down on this ground it will be your graves," she said, pulling us up onto our feet.

I was certain we would die and prayed to God I wouldn't suffer too much.

The next evening when we stopped to rest, Yusuf went to search for food.

Before leaving he pressed money into Mother's hand. She protested, but he closed her fist tightly around the paper bills. "This will allow you to buy food for a while. If I should not return, walk with the rising sun in the east at your back and toward the setting sun in the west," he said. "Avoid the main roads during the day and soon you will arrive at the border with Lebanon."

Yusuf never came back.

"Something happened to him," Mother said. "He was a fine, brave man and would not have abandoned us without good reason." She said it was now up to us to find safety.

We continued walking, watching for soldiers, and hiding when we saw trucks.

My fear was burdened with such exhaustion I could hardly stand or think. Our supply of food was gone. My mouth felt as dry as the sand under my feet and I had a terrible hunger. The pain in my leg muscles was unbearable. I stumbled and fell many times and my hands and knees were scraped and bleeding. My head felt like a stone on my shoulders and eyes like pebbles baked in the sun.

Hassan fell and would not get up.

"We will not leave you," Mother said. "If you do not get up and walk with us, then we will all die here."

Hassan stood. I took his hand and we went on. Our sleep in the cool night on hard ground was brief and fitful, leaving me in a state of near delirium the next day. Somehow my feet moved forward independent of my will. I stopped caring about whether I lived or died and thought that death might be a blessed relief. I don't know how I was able to continue. Perhaps God carried me in his arms.

In the afternoon on the fourth day, we observed a column of people walking on a road. Mother hid us behind rocks and crept closer to observe them.

She returned excited. "Those people are civilians like us," she said.

"We're going to the border crossing at Lebanon," said a man, when we approached. A woman with a bundle on her back carrying a baby invited us to join them and gave us some water and pieces of bread. The companionship of others and the small amount of food raised our spirits, although I was still exhausted and frightened.

In the evening we saw the lights of the border crossing ahead with a sign that said it was the country of Lebanon. The line to enter was long and slow-moving. I worried that they wouldn't let us in, but when we reached the gates a man in uniform allowed us to pass through.

"Salam alaikum," Mother said to him. He returned a faint smile.

I looked back at the horizon and cried when I thought of our Father. He was so kind and good, but now was gone forever. Would I ever see my country again?

Mother hugged us. "God in his mercy has preserved us," she said. "We are safe now."

They gave us blankets and we slept together on the ground. Exhausted and relieved to be safe, I fell asleep in a few moments, ignoring the cold night air, hard earth under my sore body and the emptiness of my stomach.

The next morning, people with *UN* on their uniforms asked Mother questions and gave us food, water and documents.

A woman official pointed to the top of the papers. "These are your registration numbers," she said. "Keep them with you at all times."

I looked around at the sea of tents and people from Syria. It looked as if someone had tipped our whole country upside down and emptied it of humanity. For a while we lived in a tent, but now occupy a small room in an old building. They give us cards to exchange for food. Mother got a job in a store to earn money, but they don't pay her much because she is Syrian.

"It's barely enough for us to live on," she said, "but at least we are still alive."

Mother was sick with fever for a few days and I was afraid she would die and Hassan and I would have no one in the world that cared about us, but she recovered.

People say we are fortunate to still have our lives. I am grateful to Lebanon for accepting us, but I miss my home, family and our way of life in Syria. At night before going to sleep I hear our mother weeping.

My brother Hassan is unhappy and angry.

"I hate those who killed our father and will kill them someday," he said one morning. Mother shook him and slapped his head.

"Never say you want to kill another person," she said. "All the hate in the world will not bring your father back. I will never forgive them for what they did but hate rots the soul of the person who does the hating. Hate begets itself like a spreading disease and the killing goes on and on without end. Your thirst for vengeance will destroy you. God will punish those men for their actions."

I wondered if that would ever happen.

The local Lebanese children do not want us as friends and we are kept separate from them. Some Lebanese adults call us bad names. To them we are foreigners and refugees, not human beings.

My brother and I have a place in a school, but the teachers and studies are different and the classes large. In Syria we had books and good paper to write on, but not here. We must write down everything the teacher says on pads of plain, rough paper because we cannot afford the books.

Yet, I am thankful for this classroom since it is the only thing I have in my life now. Learning is medicine for my sorrow and I work hard at my lessons. My goal is to be a teacher, return to Syria and help rebuild my country. With God's help I will accomplish my objective.

19.   MY ANGEL
By Rena Flannigan

This is the first story I ever wrote, September 2008.

For a long time I have thought of trying to write a story but did not have the time or opportunity – or even confidence to try. Now that I am almost retired and join in different classes held in Flower City Seniors Centre, I saw there was a course to learn how to write and I thought – why not? So here I am. I have always enjoyed writing letters as well as receiving them; I still prefer a letter to an email. I have letters going back to the 'dark ages' it seems. I am a pack-rat and hate to part with anything with print on it. I enjoy taking out the old letters and can see my friends again as I reread them all. We have to write about a subject each week apparently and the first subject drawn out of the pretty little bag the teacher, Jeanette, has was about an angel. How appropriate, I thought.

Over the many years I have noticed people wearing tiny angels on their jackets or coats and always thought how nice it must be to have your own personal angel to guard you and even talk to at times. I have bought my daughter and my good friend each an angel and although they are both very considerate and thoughtful people they never bought me one. Not that I gave one to get one, don't misunderstand me, just that they both thoughtful as I said but maybe they thought I am a very lucky and blessed person and don't really need 'an angel on my shoulder' to quote and old song. That I am lucky and blessed with good health, a good family and friends is a given, I doubt if there are many people in this world as blessed as I am.

I am a great believer in fate and somehow Fate brought a new friend into my life recently. We exchanged small gifts when we met, mine as a Thank You for the help I had been given by this friend and the friend in turn bought me a gift as a memento of our lovely visit together. Imagine my joy when I saw a pretty golden angel in it's package for me. Who knows, maybe I was not intended to have an angel on my shoulder before now but had to wait for someone extra special to enter my life who would give me a personal angel to wear. The friendship is new but I know it will lat a long, long time, it was just one of those rare moments we encounter as we journey along lifes path.

I treasure the angel and the thought behind the gift, I speak to it every morning and night and ask it to look out for my friend and bring good health and joy for them every day as long as they live.

2021.

For any real writer who may read this, my first effort of story telling, I copied it as it was in 2008. I thank the authors along the way, amateurs like myself, with much more talent than I had. They have helped me grow and I like to think I have learned a lot along the way. Jeanette, I appreciated the notes and comments you gave when you read my stories, to you, in particular I give thanks. They gave me incentive to carry on writing, who knows, there might be a book some day where you will be mentioned. Thank you to many others who helped as well.

20.   RIDING THE *J TRAIN*
By Ken Puddicombe

Think of the Big Apple and the mind instantly conjures images of The Rockettes and Radio City Music Hall, the lights of Times Square, and the Subway.

It was my first trip back to New York after many years and I was eager to see the results of the smart revolutionary method the Transit Authority had adopted to overcome the graffiti problem, a method that involved using new material that was both washable and paint proof.

As I sat in the *J Train* heading to Coney Island, I could see that this had worked for the greater part—the walls were now clean and free of the bizarre art which had one threatened to strangle the entire system. But now, as the doors of the carriage opened at the stations down the line, it was obvious that the artists had looked upon this as a challenge they could not ignore. The artwork had moved to the ceiling, to the pillars, and even on the advertisements hanging on the walls! It stretched my imagination: how did these modern-day Michaelangelos manage to find the opportunity and means to reach up so far to the ceiling to paint?

It was not too long before the carriage was crowded and every square foot was occupied, people bracing against the entry-exit doors and hanging on to overhead straps suspended from the roof of the carriage. I looked at the advertisements framed high on the wall. They were a mixed bunch, these ads, selling services and products I had never seen offered anywhere else.

The first one that caught my eye was over the door. It read: *Do you suffer from Anal Warts and fissures? Manhattan Medical Clinic can get rid of them through their revolutionary laser method—no surgery required.*

Directly across from me, in front of the door as the train slowly made its way on the elevated line, stood a man in black clothes, matching sneakers, and curly Afro hair. His eyes were focussed on the guy in the three-piece suit seated next to me reading, minding his own business, like so many others on the train engrossed in novels, magazines, newspapers, or had earphones plugged into cassette decks or radios.

The man in black continued to stare. He had a black wrist band on his right hand and every now and then his index finger stabbed the air in my direction, like someone on the throes of a voodoo incantation about to cast an evil spell. A black duffel bag hung on his left shoulder and he had to reposition it several times to prevent it from slipping to the floor. Just about the only thing not black about him was his pearly white teeth that flashed every time he opened his mouth to mumble something.

On my right, a woman who was already on the train when I boarded, was half-asleep, gravitating ever so closer in my direction every time her head bobbed to her chest. From the corner of my eye I saw her wake suddenly. She smiled, a wide effusive smile as she mumbled something under her breath. The, she laughed, clapped her hands as if she had been suddenly made privy to something funny, closed her eyes and nodded off again.

The Man In Black was tall, so tall that he had to stand with his head bent along the curve of the ceiling, to the point where he touched the ad on the wall. It read: *Tired of living the high life? We can help if you have a drug problem.* And right next to it: *Manhattan Footcare. Let us fix your feet right the first time.*

At the end of the aisle, next to the small cabin of the conductor, the door slowly slid open. The sign that said: *Warning. It is dangerous to walk between carriages* retreated into the door cavity and then reappeared behind the woman who entered, slowly making her way to the centre of the carriage. She stopped, a couple of feet in front of me and waved a *Daily Mirror* in the air. She said, "Ladies and gentlemen. Could I have your attention?"

A shuffling of shoes on the floor greeted her, a rustle of paper, a noticeable change in activity throughout the carriage as all heads turned towards her. She said, above the harsh clutter of the wheels on the tracks, "Please buy my newspaper. I'm being put out of my apartment. Please help me out. I appeal to you." And without waiting for a response, she continued her way to the door at the other end of the carriage, passing close to the Man In Black who pulled aside to make way for her, mumbling in an audible baritone: "Crazy woman. Why don' she leave people alone."

Still more ads on the walls. *Say goodbye to wrinkles. Competent Plastic Surgeon will give you the lift you need in life.* The one that really caught my eye next to this: *Torn ear lobes? We can fix them. Quickly. Painlessly. Cheaply.* I looked around to see how many people were really going around New York with torn ear lobes. And how in the world did they ever get that way?

The Man In Black had made his exit at the previous stop. We were now on the outskirts of the borough of Queens, coming up to the end of the elevated portion of the line, almost into Manhattan. We passed houses, apartments, businesses, all merely feet from the tracks, even closer at times as the train screeched its way around bends, sparks flying through open windows. At eye level: iron bars on windows; entrances with metal encasements for storm doors; an air conditioner hanging outside a window; a steel mesh surrounding it. Children played in hallways, people stared from open windows, curious about who was riding the train, as inquisitive as I was about who lived there. And which had come first, I wondered? Which half-crazed city planner had actually zoned apartments so close to a train line? Or which deranged engineer had thought of placing an overhead line in such proximity to a residential area?

Then below, abandoned cars in the middle of the street, stacks of tires, construction material, litter, and empty lots overgrown with weeds. In the middle of it all, an oasis: a field, lush, verdant; a green palette splattered with bright red tomatoes, purple egg plants and yellow string beans hanging from vines.

Still more signs on the train. *If you're going to do it, do it right. Use a condom. Sponsored by NY Aids Hotline.* And: *Safe abortions. No risk. The best pre and after care in Manhattan.*

We were passing a cemetery. Huge tombs sparkling white and adorned with flowers, filled the landscape. They all looked alike—the same size, same structure: arched roofs, pillars holding them up, like a miniature version of a Roman temple. And the names on the walls facing the tracks: *Zylberg, Sandberg, Isenberg.* Next to the cemetery, a Mason Works, a yard filled with precast concrete slabs, blank headstones lying around waiting to be claimed.

As we pulled into Brooklyn, into rail yards looking like Concentration Camps with barbed-wire curled in huge spirals high above street level, I thought of Stalag 17. There were even watchtowers overlooking the yard.

I took one last look at the ads on the way out. *Pregnant? We can help. NY Abortion Clinic. Free Walk In Consultation.* And: *Designer Braces. We can brighten up your smile today.* Also: *Hernias need not be a problem. Let us take the weight off your feet.* Next to it: *Show off your skin. Don't be ashamed to come into the light—NY Dermatology Clinic.* Then there was; *Tooth Savers Dental Center of NY. Don't wait for the Tooth Fairy. WE can save your tooth.* Finally: *Madame Zola. Put yourself in my hands. Fortune Telling. Palmistry—know what the future has in store for you.*

As I stepped on to the platform, with walls now sparkling clean and looking sterile, the thought struck me: Had the city really licked the problem; or had the graffiti moved within the carriages and become institutionalized?

21. PIGTAILS

By Michael Joll

I fell in love with her on my first day at primary school.

It was 1952, we were five, and in Mrs. Roberts' class, seated alphabetically by Christian name at pairs of wooden desks, twelve down one side of the classroom and twelve up the other. She sat against the wall on Mrs. Roberts' left, near the front. I sat in the second row from the back by the window.

If I moved my head, I could see her from where I sat. Her thick, blond hair, parted down the centre, sparkled with a hint of red when the sun glinted off it. Her pigtails, tied off with small, pink satin bows, reached below her shoulders.

I paid special attention when Mrs. Roberts called the register that first morning. When she called, "Catriona McKenzie," Catriona put up her hand.

"Present, Miss," she said.

And now I knew her name.

Mrs. Roberts continued around the room until she reached me and called my name, "Murray McLeod."

I put my hand up. "Present, Miss."

Catriona McKenzie swivelled in her seat and stared at me. I didn't know what to make of that look. I like to think a faint smile crossed her lips before she turned back to face the front. At any rate, now she knew my name and my heart experienced the first rush of adrenalin I can remember.

She played with the other girls in our class at lunch break, but when the time came to leave school that afternoon, Catriona stood outside the classroom door, waiting for me. From up close I noticed she had a sprinkling of freckles across her nose and cheeks and cornflower blue eyes that looked straight at me. I couldn't ignore them, or her, although that would be the proper boy response.

"You're Murray McLeod," she said.

My face burned. A bag of nerves by this time, on legs like jelly I hopped from one foot to the other. I needed to pee badly.

"I know where you live. I saw you leave your house this morning, and I followed you to school."

By this time a queue had formed behind me, so I stepped aside to let my classmates pass. Some gave me knowing looks. A couple of the girls made Xs with their fingers and mouthed kisses. I ignored them while I searched for a hole to crawl into and hide.

"They're jealous," Catriona said after the last passed through the doorway. "Because I'm talking to you and they want to. They told me so at break."

Mrs. Roberts had left. The other boys in the class didn't care if they left me alone to talk to the prettiest girl, not just in the school, or Invercargill, but probably the whole of New Zealand.

"You can walk home with me," she said. "My mother says a lady never walks unacc…" She tried it again. "Unaccom… *Alone.*" She glanced meaningfully at me.

"I need to go," I said, and dashed to the boys' toilets. When I re-emerged, Catriona still stood by the classroom door, waiting for me.

I smiled, hesitantly. She handed me her satchel. I gathered I was meant to carry it. I slung it over my shoulder. I carried my own in my hand.

In that manner, we walked home that early February afternoon. By home, I mean my house, a small bungalow behind a low hedge and white painted wood fence. I had my hand on the garden gate and was about to shrug her satchel off my shoulder and give it to her when she said, "I live two streets away, Murray." I remembered my manners in time and took my hand off the gate. Catriona smiled, and that adrenalin rush hit me again. I wanted to be with her forever.

"Can I walk you all the way home?" I asked. "Will your mother mind if she sees you with me?"

"No. Mummy would expect it of a gemmelman."

I walked with her the two streets to her house, a bungalow on a corner lot. Her mother came down the path to meet us. I stood at the edge of the lawn not knowing what was expected of me.

"This is Murray, Mummy," she said. "We're in Mrs. Roberts' class. Murray's going to walk to school and back with me every day. He doesn't mind." She turned to me and said, pointedly, "Do you, Murray?"

Scarlet-faced, I nodded and mumbled, "I don't mind, Mrs. McKenzie."

"Do you live close by, Murray? I wouldn't want Catriona to put you out."

"One street away."

"Two," Catriona said. "But it's on the way."

"That's right, Mrs. McKenzie. And I don't mind, honest."

*

We walked to and from school every day for the rest of the school year. Along with half the class, Catriona caught chicken pox a few days before the Christmas holiday and missed a week of school. She gave it to me too, and I spent Christmas and the next week in quarantine. Once my exile was over, the itch had gone and the scabs had dried, Mrs. McKenzie invited me to their house for the afternoon. I saw Catriona for the first time after the longest three weeks of my life.

"I picked the scab," were Catriona's first words as she pointed to a small pit centred on her forehead. "Mummy says I'll be scarred for life, and no one will want to marry me, or even kiss me, ever."

"I didn't notice," I said, hoping she believed me. The small scar was the first thing I saw when I stood close enough to feel the heat rising from her body. "And I'm sure someone will want to kiss you one day."

She studied her sandals. "Will you?" she said, scuffing at the dirt.

Catriona was smart, at the top of the class in everything. I preferred rugby and cricket. I decided the smart thing to do was to play dumb. In case. Of what, I didn't know. I was six. "Will I what?"

"Ever want to kiss me?" She looked up and I saw tears glisten in her eyes. "One day?"

I glanced over my shoulder at the deserted front garden. "I don't know. When?"

"Today? Now?"

She leaned forward with her arms stretched behind her back and closed her eyes. Our lips touched, barely grazing before I pulled back. I had never kissed a girl before. It wasn't so bad. She opened her eyes before I could wipe my mouth with the back of my hand. Tears spilled down her cheeks. "Properly," she said.

I searched the street for witnesses. A lawnmower clacked in a garden behind a house somewhere; otherwise, the neighbourhood appeared deserted. Satisfied that we were the only two people in all of Invercargill, I drew

Catriona gently to me, like I had seen them do once in a film. Perhaps Catriona had seen the same film because unspoken, our lips touched again and we held each other close enough that I smelled her soap on her skin and the scent of her shampoo in her hair. This time our kiss lasted for seconds, minutes, hours—I didn't count; I didn't care. I had wanted to kiss Catriona since that first day in Mrs. Roberts' class, and Catriona had granted my wish.

Too soon, with a final kiss, we broke away, fearful that someone would see us. Catriona took my hand in hers. "Let's go into the back garden. Mummy will bring us some Coke and some biscuits and we can sit on the swing by the pool."

That seemed like a better idea than any I had. She led me around the side of the house to the in-ground pool at the rear. We sat on the swing, sometimes talking, but most of the time in silence, holding hands. We didn't kiss again that afternoon; there didn't seem a need or a reason. When Catriona's father came home from work, I left.

"Come again, Murray, as often as you like," Mrs. McKenzie said. "Catriona doesn't seem to have any interest in playing with anyone else. And bring your swimming trunks. Catriona loves to swim and it seems a shame not to take advantage of the glorious weather. It won't last forever."

*

I went away to boarding school in Christchurch when I was eleven but we spent the school holidays together without skipping a beat. We moved easily from childhood through adolescence to adulthood. Catriona won a scholarship to the University of Otago and Cambridge University offered me a place, which I accepted.

A week before I was due to leave for England, the dam burst.

"There's no point seeing each other again," she said with ice in her voice. "You're going away. So am I."

"It's only three years," I said.

"Three or thirty," she snapped. "No difference. It's been exhausting pretending everything's still the same. It's not. We've grown apart already. We'll be strangers in three years."

"I…"

"There's no point discussing it." She took a step back from me. I reached for her hand. She pulled it behind her back. "Don't," she said. "You'd better leave. Now."

She brushed past me and opened the front door. August rain slanted down and ricocheted off the path. "Now," she repeated.

Confused, I grabbed my raincoat from the hall stand. "But…"

"Go," she said, and there was no arguing with the adamant look in her eyes. "Don't phone. Don't write. I won't go to the airport to see you off."

As I passed her I tried to kiss her one last time. She turned her cheek and flattened her body against the wall in the narrow hall. "Don't touch me," she said.

She closed the door behind me but not before I said, "I'll be back one day." I don't think either of us believed it.

I walked home in the rain; history, a memory if she thought of me at all. The starter boyfriend. Discarded. Moved on. She hadn't even said goodbye.

It hurt.

*

After university, I returned to New Zealand and joined the bank in Auckland. By the time I turned thirty, I'd earned a title beneath my name on the door of an office with real walls from floor to ceiling, and a large window looking out over the three-storey atrium, the focal point of the main downtown branch.

One lunchtime I saw her, Catriona, waiting in line at a teller's wicket. A surge of adrenalin like an electric shock hit me. She didn't look up, but I knew it could only be her: the same fair hair in braids, a shade or two darker now, and a little longer than I remembered, but still tied off with bows. As slim as ever, she wore a grey skirt, white blouse, and a navy windbreaker. In the artificial light the jacket, like her hair, glistened from the drizzle outside. Her transaction completed, Catriona turned and left the building.

I called the teller aside. "Deposit, or withdrawal?" I asked.

"Deposit, Mr. McLeod."

"May I see the cheque?"

"Is there a problem?"

"I hope not," I said. "Did you compare the signature on the endorsement against the   specimen on her application form?"

"Yes, Mr. McLeod. That account hasn't been computerized yet." She handed me the cheque. It had Catriona's name and address printed on the top left-hand corner, along with a phone number. Still McKenzie I noted. I memorized the address and handed the cheque back.

At the end of the day, I drove to the address on Catriona's cheque, a small block of flats in a bland suburban neighbourhood. I parked around the corner and waited under the awning of a café to escape the rain. I eased my weight from one foot to the other, jingling the loose change in my trouser pocket while I summoned the courage to cross the road and ring her doorbell. Nearly fourteen years-worth of butterflies flitted around my stomach.

Chilled and hunched into my raincoat, I convinced myself this was a bad idea. Catriona had made it clear she didn't want to see me again. She had her life to lead and it didn't involve me. By the time the *Southern Cross* deposited me in England, like her, I had moved on. I thought of her from time to time but that was all. Go home, I told myself. Now. She doesn't want to see you. Don't embarrass her.

While I dithered, a bus drew up and stopped in front of the block of flats. When the bus pulled away, I saw Catriona on her way to the front door of the building. She stopped, fished her door keys out from her handbag, and unlocked the door. She pushed the door open and disappeared into the lobby. I gave her a few minutes, then crossed the road, in an instant five years old again and in Mrs. Roberts' class. And Catriona was the most beautiful girl in the world.

I stabbed the buzzer for her flat with a finger. I had no idea what I planned to say to her, but I knew one thing for sure: just like that first day at school, I needed to pee.

The tinny sound of Catriona's voice through the speaker echoed around the lobby.

"Catriona?" I waited a second. "It's Murray McLeod, from Invercargill."

A lengthy silence followed. I was about to turn away when the door unlocked with a loud clunk. I looked for a lift but I couldn't find one. I climbed the stairs, and when I reached her floor, I checked for a sign to indicate which way to turn for her flat. At that moment, a door opened at the end of the corridor. A pigtailed head poked around the corner. She waved, beckoning me. I stopped in front of her door. We regarded each other in silence while recognition sunk in and the years evaporated.

Catriona smiled and said, "Come in."

I stepped inside.

"I hope you don't mind the mess. It's the maid's day off." She laughed the way I remembered.

"Mine too," I said.

I heard a commotion, and a moment later two nearly identical girls with puzzled, barely teenage faces, appeared hesitantly at the end of the short hallway.

I gave a small wave. "I'm Murray McLeod."

"We know," said one.

"Mum told us," said the other.

Catriona gave a light cough. "Megan."

Megan raised her hand.

"And Kate." Catriona choked back a sob. Tears spilled down her cheeks. I wrapped my arms around her and clasped her head to my chest. She clung to me with a fierceness I had never known. She snuggled in my arms until, as we had so many years ago on the street in front of her house, she untangled herself from my clutches and gave me a watery, tear-filled kiss.

"Our daughters."

22.   INVADED

By Raymond Holmes

"You must be joking Grandpa."

Blank stares on the children's faces when Gordon told them he didn't have computers at his first job.

"Not even calculators on your phones?"

"We didn't have cell phones to equip with calculators or anything else."

Their faces formed an *I don't believe you* look.

He started to explain slide rules and long-handed mathematical calculations but gave up when their eyes glazed over.

"How could you do any work, Grandpa?" one said.

"Everyone used pens, pencils and paper back then. People could write. In fact, penmanship was a school subject and there was a source of pride in good handwriting."

The youngest pointed at her iPad. "We just type on the screen."

Students relied on computers now. Schools didn't teach cursive writing or how to tell the time using an analog clock. How will future generations sign contracts and passports? Gordon supposed they'll just make some mark like early aboriginal people did when white men pushed documents they couldn't read in front of their faces and swindled them out of their land.

"How did you play games without a computer or X-Box?" one granddaughter said.

"Back then, the only available games were board games, cards, and sports. You actually had to play with other real, live people—sometimes outdoors."

"Sounds boring, Grandpa," said the youngest one, wrinkling her face.

Gordon was convinced his grandchildren would be part of a lost generation, bereft of essential life skills and at the mercy of a big brother computer for their every need. He read that some experts believe children's obsession with these devices is a damaging, digital drug. Their cautions are largely ignored, except ironically by some Silicon Valley engineers who won't let their children use them or at least severely limit the time spent. What did they know that everyone else didn't?

Travelling reminded him that the most mundane and personal actions had been computerized commencing with his self-check-in at the airport. Taps and toilets in public washrooms dispensed water automatically when used. On a trip to Europe Gordon and his wife Jane encountered washrooms that automatically sanitized toilet seats after each use and announced in several languages, "Remember to wash your hands." He'd heard that someone had invented computerized toilet accessories that could automatically clean your private parts. Oh, the damage a malfunction of one of those accessories could do. Ouch.

Gordon's home was filled with annoying computers. He wasn't much of a cook and their computerized kitchen electric range didn't help his culinary abilities. He read the manual several times, but always forgot what buttons on the touchpad did what. It really wasn't his fault that the roasting time accidently got set to twenty hours instead of two hours one afternoon. First time he'd had prime rib charred to perfection.

One day two of the smooth-top burners on the stove wouldn't work.

The *Appliances R' Us* man shook his head. "It'll cost seven hundred dollars to repair," he said.

"But we only paid nine hundred for it," said Gordon.

"Individual burners aren't serviceable. I'll need to change out the entire top."

Gordon used to buy replacement coil burners for their old stove at the hardware store for $12.95 each. Now, unlike the good old days, computerized items are discarded and replaced with new ones, not repaired.

Gordon clicked the remote for his fifty-five-inch satellite television and saw the screen come to life with a commercial for dental whitener. The programming, courtesy of a computer orbiting far above earth, cost $89.00 per month plus tax. Smart hardware, but expensive, dumbed-down programming with hundreds of redundant channels in every language interspersed with stupid commercials every few minutes. His first television used rabbit ears, the programming was free and more entertaining, and the set could be repaired at reasonable cost, unlike his current one. When this fifty-five-inch behemoth went belly up, they'd have to place it at the curb and pay the city forty dollars to take it away.

Their computerized home alarm system proved to be a royal nuisance because it couldn't tell the difference between Simba, their sixteen-pound cat and a burglar, when they were away.

"We should cancel the service," Gordon said after hearing that home security systems and even baby monitors could be hacked and perverts anywhere in the world could view your family's most intimate moments.

"That only happens to other people," Jane said.

At least keeping their car in the garage prevented thieves from stealing it using a computer to clone the keyless fob. That happened to a neighbour.

In October, Jane gave Gordon an iPad for his birthday.

"Tell me again why I need this thing, honey?"

"So you can stay up-to-date and be connected."

That word *connected* again. "But I have a cell phone and computer for that, he said."

"The phone's for when you're out and about. The iPad will do everything the laptop will and is more convenient. You can sell the computer."

Gordon would rather get rid of his sixty dollar a month cell phone. Every two seconds it beeped with an inane Facebook post, advertisement, or message of what was happening in some remote corner of the world. Constant availability by cell phone was like having a pebble stuck in your shoe. Perhaps she had a point about the laptop.

Jane continued. "You need the iPad to stay connected at mealtimes, to use in bed before you go to sleep, and when you wake up in the morning."

Her statement contained the fodder for a joke about marital life and the boudoir, but he refrained. Arguing with a woman was impossible.

It took two hours on the phone to get the iPad working properly and its on-screen keypad wasn't word processor-friendly like the laptop. Gordon purchased a seventy-dollar Bluetooth accessory keyboard for it, but the device stopped working after one week.

"I wish you'd throw away all your music CD's and get an iPod," Jane said, adding, "get rid of all your books too. You can download them all to a Kindle Reader."

"Over my dead body," Gordon snapped. Hopefully no one would tell her that an iPad could play music *and* download books too.

Gordon used the iPad Jane gave him to read the news every morning. No point in having the $429.00 plus tax cost go to waste.

One day at his 10:30 a.m. coffee break, three articles popped up. The first made Gordon laugh, the second made him cringe, and the last made him wonder if the days of humans were numbered.

The first stated COMPUTERIZED CYBER PETS ALL THE RAGE IN JAPAN. It went on to describe how the Japanese become emotionally attached to these artificial animal companions and become bereaved if they break down. People who repair them are called Cyber Vets.

The article listed all their advantages over real, live creatures, most of them laughable except for the elimination of expensive pet food. Nothing was mentioned about litter pans or shedding fur. Maybe those cyber-pets *are* designed to be realistic creatures—peeing, pooping and shedding fur over the furniture. Computers had convinced people they didn't need real animals for pets anymore.

The second post announced COMPUTERS MAKE DRIVERLESS CARS A REALITY.

Gordon recalled his recent exasperating conversations with the annoying female voices of his car's driver interface system and GPS and tried to imagine a driverless chariot bringing him home along a major highway in a raging winter blizzard. Would a matter-of-fact voice announce, "This hill is too icy for me to drive up," or "You are now stuck in a snowbank—sorry. Distance to home by foot is X kilometers. Wear a tuque and scarf."

The last article on the iPad astonished him. DUTCH COMPANY TO OPEN CYBER BROTHEL. For a price, patrons could have sex with computerized life-like silicone dolls in private cubicles. Gordon's mind tumbled with thoughts of what that experience might be like. Would these computerized doxies smile and suggest new techniques? Would he hear feedback on his performance in a voice reminiscent of the GPS lady's critical remarks concerning his driving habits and wrong turns? Would condoms be optional? He couldn't help wondering about an in-use malfunction or who was going to clean these faux women at the end of the day. Thinking about the latter issue made him nauseous. Hopefully the company would maintain insurance in case their customers were injured or contracted STD's.

After worming their way into every aspect of our lives, it seemed that computers were even going to service our libidos now. Having already killed millions of jobs, they were now going to put the oldest profession out of work. What frontiers were left for processors to conquer? The article concluded that this was part of the first wave of AAI. Gordon looked that acronym up and a knot formed in the pit of his stomach. The definition: *Advanced Artificial intelligence* that would make computers even smarter and able to take over what remained of the sovereignty of our lives.

Computerized everything and computer spawn including on-line scams, spoofing, phishing, viruses, malware and ransomware were driving Gordon nuts. Any day now he'd snap. With his luck he'd end up in an institution staffed by computerized android attendants and taking digital pills.

Darn, the WiFi's down. He'd have to go upstairs to ask Jane a question.

23.   A BAT IN MY BELFRY
By Rena Flannigan

Just as I was fading into a deep sleep, I heard a noise in my bedroom, and it confused me. I knew it was not a romantic interlude in my life because I was alone in my bed. It sounded like something scratching but since it is normally very quiet, it took a few minutes to try to figure out what the noise could be at 2:45 in the morning.

I opened one eye slightly and imagined I saw a shadow flitting around the ceiling going from room to room. I don't have screens on my windows and sleep with the bedroom window open about five inches—winter and summer. Living on the seventh floor, I am normally not bothered with bugs, so this was a whole new thing to figure out.

This scratching sound was a whole new experience, I thought it can't be a bird at this time of night then thought it might be a bat, and indeed it was. It appeared to have a wingspan of at least eight inches, not small by any means to have in the bedroom. After opening the other windows as far as I could, I was hoping that the bat would find its way out the same way as when it came in. I was hoping for the best—no luck. I was tired but I lay watching it fly around for a bit—mostly it flew close to the ceiling.

Soon, however, it was back in my bedroom which I was not happy about, but being so tired I figured it would be okay if we spent the night together, my bat and I. It flew around, up and down and once or twice, it looked like it might dive-bomb me. I decided if it did not bother me, I would not bother it. Strangely enough, I was not afraid, had I been it would have been the couch for the night for me.

In the morning I went bat hunting, could not find it anywhere and felt relieved hoping it had gone out again. How, I did not care—that it was not there was the important thing for me by now. I went about my day and forgot about the bat. Imagine my shock when, after being out for a few hours in the evening, the first thing I encountered as I entered my home was…the bat! What to do now? I was alone with no way of opening the windows wider for it to exit, but it didn't; instead it flitted around again so I decided to call my daughter and my son-in-law. I wasn't sure they could do much, but three heads are better than one old lady who can't reach anything high. And it was high—in a corner of the blind near the ceiling and being short I knew I could not reach it.

I sent a text to my daughter and got no reply. Last resort, I called security in the lobby. I explained my situation and we spoke back and forth as to what to try for a solution. Great I thought, now my mind is going into overdrive. I slept with the bat last night, but I had no intention of doing the same tonight. Just as I hung up the phone it rang again, it was my daughter calling. She had sent a text saying she was on her way and called me as well to ask what was going on. I had made a cup of tea so decided that I would drink it while it was hot and think seriously what I would do next. Tea is a good pacifier and helps to clear the brain, I find.

Knock, knock, my two heroes arrived. The bat did not stand a chance with these two on the warpath I thought, but silly me thinking this. We saw the bat on a blind minding its own business, so all these two brave characters had to do was stun the bat with a floor brush, put him in a plastic bag and dispose of him into the night. Every light in the condo was lit supposedly to drive the bat towards the dark window. Hmm, not so easy after all. It flew around the living room and we were looking all over for him, spotting him perched on a cupboard door in the kitchen. Imagine these two trying to figure out a mode of attack if you will.

I finally said, "give me the blooming brush," and trapped the poor bat against the cupboard door. The problem was that there is a space between the top of the door and the ceiling so off the bat went again. Once more the chase was on.

The bat did not take kindly to being chased, and certainly not to being hit with the bristles of a brush. It took off into the bedroom again. Now the field of battle had been minimized. We closed the doors and made the area much more confined. The bat settled on the blinds up in a corner of the window, my two heroes fiddled with the brush wondering how to attack and catch it. My son-in-law tried to stun him with the brush and the same time my daughter was supposed to catch the bat in a plastic bag as it fell.

While these two debated who was the biggest hunter, the bat flew off the blind. I wish you could have heard my daughter screaming her head off, accompanied with a few expletives I didn't know my daughter knew! She was terrified and ran to mummy to be protected, I liked that—it had been years since I had been able to comfort her. *A fine kettle of fish this is* crossed my mind, neither one of them was capable of the *big hunt*. This gave the bat a chance to crawl under the bedroom door and escape.

Perched high again on the door to the main hallway he became a perfect target for these two big-game hunters. Since the bat was by the door one of them opened the door enough to send the bat into the hallway. Watching them going into the hall themselves a few minutes later was hilarious, both of them peeking out, ready to duck if the bat came near. It did once and my daughter screamed again. I wonder what the people in the building thought about these terrifying screams. Apparently, the bat had flown near them as they waited for the elevator. They took the stairs instead and left the bat in the hallway.

For us this was the end of the bat without his bat mobile. Now, the poor animal was probably going to roam the hallway all night and I hoped everyone's door had a tight fit into the doorframe so that the bat won't go for a walk under a crack as it did to get out of my bedroom. I hoped also that it did not enter someone else's home or find the way to my door again.

Addendum: my daughter told me later that she had told her friend: "If my mum had been wearing a skirt, I would have crawled underneath it to try to get back into her womb." She is such a brave girl – NOT!

24.   ON THE BOARDWALK

By Ken Puddicombe

At the end of the line on the *J Train* to Coney Island was a platform leading to a flight of stairs into a tunnel.

I walked through the tunnel and kept on walking, with disbelief. It was as if I was exiting through a bomb shelter—dank, dark and depressing, pools of water on the ground, drops seeping from cracks overhead, a few functioning lights hanging from the ceiling attempting to relieve the gloomy atmosphere. But no graffiti.

The passage seemed to have no end in sight.

Finally, ahead in the distance, a light, then a wide-open corridor with turnstiles to the street. But the place reeked of urine, feces and decrepitude. Then, as I came outside, the smell of the ocean, but more like a fish market late in the afternoon when the last remaining fish lay unsold on concrete slabs.

Onto the Boardwalk. Planks suspended over the beach, wide as a modern highway, stretching as far as the eye could see, the Atlantic on one side, Coney Island on the other. And how it had all changed. I recalled better times, so many years ago, people flocking to the beach, rides for the kids, music in the background.

The rides were still there, but a far cry from the ones I had known back then.

With my video camera strung around my neck, I sauntered along the Boardwalk, trying to recreate a visit over twenty years ago. But those were different times.

I passed people on the Boardwalk. A man pulling a transparent plastic bag behind him. He stopped at the nearby garbage can, rifled through it, pulled out two Coke cans and stuffed them into the bag. The man sleeping on the nearby bench with his hand over his head never stirred at the rattling of the cover of the garbage can.

Then, as I looked at an abandoned ride, its charred ruins still standing high in the air, the loops and curls now rusted and warped from a fire that must have taken its toll, a voice rang out: "Hey you."

I turned in the direction of the voice, a spontaneous reaction, due more to curiosity rather than any realization that someone would actually know me in this area. What could the person in the passing wheelchair possibly want with me, anyhow?

"Don't you take my picture with that camera," he snarled, through thick lips and broken discoloured teeth. "Nobody takes my picture without my permission."

He slowed down as he passed me, moving the chair by turning the wheels with his hands, one after the other as they started from the back and brought the wheels up to the front then repeated the action. The tyres were flat, the wheels rusted in spots along the rims, the spokes bent and warped out of shape in places. He wore blue jeans cut above the knees, his spindly, shrivelled-up legs lifeless on the footrest several inches above the ground.

I kept him in sight as he wheeled close bye. He turned his head to look at me, glaring through narrow slits, his eyes barely visible in his puffed-up face. His face was black and blue, lacerations all over.

I looked at him but said nothing as he wheeled his way down the Boardwalk and I wondered: Had so much resentment, hostility built up over his disability that he had now turned bully, or was he trying to make up for his defect by this grand show of force and bravado?

An amusement park lay to the west of the Boardwalk. I could hear the sing along tune of the merry-go-round, saw the Ferris-wheel tumbling around high in the sky, smelled the hot dogs and French fries filtering even above the salt in the air. I decided to take my break but first I had to use the washroom.

I asked at the hot-dog counter for directions to the washroom. The clerk pointed to the Ferris wheel and told me to follow the signs. An arrow led to a junction: the right pointed to the Ferris-wheel, the left was blocked by a turnstile. A teenage boy stood behind the turnstile, a pouch in front of his crotch hanging from a belt. He had his hands inside the pouch; he pulled them out hastily when I approached and held them to his sides, guilt in his look.

A woman rushed up with a little boy in tow. She held the boy by his shoulders, steering him right, then left, uncertainty and panic showing in her face, pain in the boy's. Then, she read the sign over the turnstile, the one that posted the twenty-five cents fare for entry. She said, "Ooh," rumbled through her handbag and came up with a dollar and handed it to the attendant who made change from his pouch.

I let and the boy and mother get ahead as I inserted my quarter into the turnstile—their need seemed far more urgent than mine.

The gent's washroom was a no larger than a Johnny-On-the spot facility. I squeezed through the narrow door, closed it behind me and pushed the small bolt in place. There was barely enough room to turn around to face the urinal, and in the summer heat I had to hold my breath as the putrid odour rose and assaulted my nostrils. While I held my breath, I looked around. The edifice was nothing more than an assembly of concrete blocks hastily slapped together with mortar, the bricks protruding unevenly and painted with whitewash. I washed my hands in the sink no larger than a bird bath, turned around to leave, my brain reeling from the lack of oxygen.

In the corridor leading to the exit, a sign: *We take pride in these facilities. Anyone found defacing them will be prosecuted.*

I walked back to the Boardwalk, heading for the jetty—an extension of about one hundred yards into the Atlantic, and which appeared to be a popular spot. I was curious about the reason. Had the people on the jetty also paid a visit to the washroom?

The entire rail around the jetty was lined with people fishing—rods hanging over the rail, lines leading out to the water ten feet below. Men, women children, entire families with picnic hampers; people pulling in small nets, a small boy pulling up a trap with a crab inside. There was an air of holiday frivolity about. Where did these people come from? Were they earnest about fishing or merely doing it for pleasure?

I walked over to the boy who was gingerly extracting a crab from a cage. Behind him, was smaller cage with half a dozen small crabs.

I said, "Looks as if you're having a good catch."

The boy smiled, shrugged and said, "No habla Inglis," then returned to his trap.

Below, riding the waves, an older man swam towards the jetty, through the muddy water with an oil slick floating on top. The extreme end of the jetty, the farthest point beyond which the Atlantic lay, was wet. Dirty water spewed from a broken pipe. A mother ran over to her son who was drinking with cupped hands. She smacked him on his head and said, "That's not drinking water."

I walked back towards Coney Island, passing by the sideshow where a few people stood outside the entrance. A man dressed like a Ringmaster, bullhorn in hand, announced the attraction: "Come see the Snake Lady and the Jungle Man," he urged the crowd. "Only half price for this show. Give me one dollar and see the Snake Lady do her famous trick..." and next to him was a lady with a huge boa constrictor wrapped around her body. She held the snake by the neck and stroked it. Screams and loud music came from inside the tent. The black family in front of me stood by the entrance, trying to decide if it was worth the price of admission.

I passed more people on the way. A vendor walking by with a huge cooler on a dolly. "Get your cool drinks while you can. Beer-Miller, Coke..." He asked me something in Spanish and I replied with one of the few words I know, "Nada."

People lying on the benches or sitting braced against the side shows or hovels, watching life go by. A man whistling at a lady: "Hey, good looking, where you from? Wanna go out tonight?"

I was standing by the rail at the end of the Boardwalk, taping the ship heading out in the Atlantic, wondering perhaps, if its destination was South America, to another shore where the ocean lapped on a coastline in Georgetown, Guyana, a land I'd immigrated from many years prior.

"Hey, you, did you take my picture?" That voice again.

He came at me from behind this time. I hadn't seen him on my walk to the jetty. Where had he been? Had he lain in ambush, waiting for me so that he could pounce again?

I ignored him and walked away.

"If you take my picture I'll break the camera around your effing neck," he shouted.

He wheeled the chair around me and while I strolled away, he circled like a rabid dog, looking for an opening, but keeping a safe enough distance, perhaps not sure of my reaction.

"Leh me see that camera. I wanna make sure you don't have me in there," he said, as the circle narrowed.

"No you, don't," I said, nodding and glaring at him, no trace of amusement or tolerance evident in my voice or demeanour. "You're not touching this camera." And I swung the camera on the strap around my right hand, just so he could be sure of my intention. "The only way you're going to take this camera, is if I wrap it around your head," I said.

"Nobody takes my effing picture without my permission," he said.

He must have sensed the disgust in my voice and been unwilling to test my patience. He aimed his wheelchair in the direction of the jetty and left, mumbling and looking back at me with dagger-like glances. Now, I felt he was acting more like the schoolyard bully than a rabid dog as he sucked his teeth and headed away.

As he pulled away, I shouted, just loud enough for him to hear: "Who the hell wants to take you picture anyway? What makes you think you're so special?" But he said nothing, did not even give me another glance.

I'd had enough of the Boardwalk for another twenty years, perhaps. Maybe the next time I returned things would be different, closer to what they were twenty years ago, something like what I'd always envisioned when I heard the song by the Drifters.

I headed back, reluctant to join the subway.

25.   SIKANDER

By Michael Joll

"My mother was a whore, Hewitson."

General, Viscount Sinclair, KGB, DSO, grinned at the younger man squirming in the leather armchair opposite.

"Not a dishonest, native Bengali whore, you understand," Sinclair said. "Not one who rents out her favours by the half-hour and leaves her unfortunate client with a permanent souvenir of his ill-considered dalliance."

Colonel Hewitson winced and sat upright on the edge of the deep chair.

"Unlike yours," General Sinclair said, "my mother was a penniless Cornish woman of very modest birth named Grace Hopkins. She stepped ashore in Calcutta some years before my birth, bent on seeking adventures away from the scrutiny of family, and on snaring a husband, suitable or otherwise. Not necessarily in that order."

Sinclair poured a glass of claret from the silver jug at his elbow. "Pour yourself one," he said, nudging the jug across the table separating them in the cavernous Whitehall office. "Today is my ninetieth birthday and I'll be damned if I'll celebrate alone. I laid in a dozen cases of the '29 Lafitte last year. With the way Chamberlain kowtowed to that wretched little Austrian corporal it seemed the prudent thing to do. We both know what it will come to. The only uncertainty is how long it will last this time."

"It can't be worse than the last one," Colonel Hewitson said quietly.

"That's what they always say before the balloon goes up. Misplaced optimism, I call it. Overestimating our strengths and underestimating theirs." Sinclair took a solid swallow of his wine and put his glass down. "Not a bad drop," he said, wiping a few red beads from his white moustache. He settled back in his wing-back chair and squinted at Hewitson over the rim of his glass. A slight movement in the shadow of the room caught the latter's eye.

"Ignore the amanuensis, dear boy," Sinclair said. "You will need to rely on him and his scribblings when you come to write my authorized biography."

"Your biography?"

"Precisely. That is the purpose of this meeting."

Colonel Hewitson opened his mouth, uttered, "Oh," and closed it again.

"No doubt you are flattered that I should have chosen you above all others."

Hewitson cast a glance around the office and fidgeted. He opened his mouth again, then closed it without making a sound. After a lengthy silence, he took a deep breath and said, "Indeed, General, though I'm hardly qualified."

"You can receive help with the writing. Any ink-stained wretch in Fleet Street will be only too glad to get his name on the cover as the ghostwriter. But I chose you because I can rely on you to retell faithfully all that I shall disclose."

"I see," Hewitson said, with doubt creeping into the two slowly uttered words.

"Mine is a long life and misspent from the start. Rather like Kim's."

"Who's?"

"Kim. The reprehensible young lad in Kipling's book of the same name. I met him, you know."

"Who?"

"Kipling. While I was stationed in Lahore before the war. A newspaper Johnny. I think he must have got the idea for the book from my childhood exploits. Did quite well with it, I'm told. Have you read it?"

"No."

"Neither have I. But that's by the by. My earliest memories don't begin, though, until I was eight, which was when the Sepoys mutinied in eighteen fifty-seven. Bad show. You probably read about it."

Sinclair looked up to see his newly-appointed biographer nodding his agreement. "Ungrateful lot, the Sepoys. But what can one expect, having to rely on foreign troops? Not accustomed to proper British Army discipline. It had to happen eventually I suppose."

"What?"

"The mutiny. Inevitable."

Sinclair selected a Corona from the humidor on the table in front of him and lit it. Hewitson watched him in silence. An invitation to enjoy a Corona was not forthcoming. For a while Sinclair puffed on the cigar, watching the blue rings drift towards the high ceiling, ignoring the man opposite.

Hewitson uttered a deferential cough.

Sinclair sat up. "Where were we?"

"Your mother, the whore. Or the Indian Mutiny."

Sinclair leaned back again and closed his eyes.

"My father was on the Viceroy's staff at the time. Not much of a father, you understand, from what I'm told, but possessing a handy social title which, along with money, was what my mother wanted."

The General examined the glowing tip of his cigar with approval.

"Good-looking white women of flexible virtue were in short supply in India in those days, Hewitson. Still are, probably and for several years my mother was in high demand. She worked her way quickly up the social ladder and settled her hooks into my father. I don't believe he saw further career advancement, at least not while married to a woman such as my mother if indeed they married. I gather that there was a civil ceremony of questionable probity shortly after the announcement that my mother was expecting me. They parted company soon after my birth. My mother conveniently provided the grounds for the divorce in exchange for a minor maharajah's annual bribe payment. I am my mother's son in some respects."

He grew up in Calcutta, Sinclair said, absorbing Hindi and Bengali as easily as he did English. By age eight he moved among both whites and natives with ease, and with scant guidance from his mother who still had a living to pursue. "My mother insisted on calling me Charles, though I preferred Sikander, the name that the servants, their urchin children and my Indian friends bestowed upon me. It comes from my third Christian name, Alexander. Appropriate in some respects. Sikander is the name they gave to Alexander the Great when he invaded India."

"When was that?"

"I forget exactly when. A long time ago. Ancient Greek fellow, if I remember. Now, don't interrupt."

*

Noon on New Year's Eve 1857, Sinclair recalled, found him on the pavement in front of Fernandes' Spice Emporium on Elphinstone Street while Gulameer, his mother's bearer, haggled with the ghari driver over the fare owed. The small boy waited in bored silence for the negotiations to finish while the blinkered old nag between the shafts deposited the contents of its recent feed and the pungent stream of urine that followed into the dust at its hooves. The horse shivered its skin around an open sore where the harness chafed an old callus. The flinch dispersed the handful of flies that had settled to feast on the raw, oozing mess and to lay their eggs in the ragged pink edges of the decaying flesh.

Young Sikander had grown up with the familiar smells of Calcutta; the stink of open sewers, the stench of dung, the smell of horse sweat in harness leather, and the unique aroma of the ghari's leather upholstery. Inculcated from infancy to accept the reality of the harshness of life inflicted on those low-caste natives marooned at the bottom of a ladder devoid of rungs, the boy showed no interest in the plight of either the ghari driver or his bony mare.

An aromatic medley of ground spices wafted into Sikander's nostrils. He turned his attention to the colourful mounds of spices in a dozen flat baskets lying in Fernandes' open shop window; bright yellow turmeric, the pale ochre of ground ginger, brown shades of cardamom, cumin and lemon-scented coriander, of khaki garam masala, of fenugreek, nutmeg and allspice, and almost black cloves from Zanzibar. String upon string of dried red chillies hung in long chains from poles near the door, adding their pungent, eye-watering aroma to the mix.

The noisy ritual of the pantomime between the bearer and the ghari driver reached its conclusion, unsatisfactory to either party. Sikander watched the horse and ghari clop down the street in response to the driver's lazy application of whip. He looked up at the sun at its zenith in response to his stomach's growl. "Tiffin time, Gulameer," he said in his piping voice.

The bearer ignored him. "Just a pakora, Gulameer. Or a samosa. Please. I'm hungry."

But Gulameer had his head cocked slightly as if listening intently to something Sikander could not hear and paid no attention to the boy's plea. Soon Sikander heard it too; the faint, distant hum of flies or bees.

"What is it?"

"Shh!" Gulameer whispered, putting a finger to his lips as he looked around uncertainly. "Come," he said, taking the small boy by the hand. "It is not safe to stay here. There are men, many men, bent on mischief."

He led Sikander down a side alley between the spice shop and a sari store. In the shadows of the narrow alley, they stopped, listening to the sound of the distant, angry crowd fill the noon air. A horse neighed. A gunshot rang out.

Gulameer and the small boy set off at a trot through the maze of dark alleys. Moments later, an explosion rocked the buildings around them, blowing glass shards down the alley where they had stood moments before. A pall of black smoke billowed above the rooftops of the squat buildings on either side of them as they picked up their pace.

"It is much more better if they do not find us here," Gulameer panted as he stopped briefly to check the sun to get his bearings. "Come," he said, and took the boy by the hand again, setting off at a faster pace.

Hemmed in by the walls of low mud hovels, the staccato slapping of Sikander's sandals and the heavy crump of Gulameer's boots on the beaten earth of the narrow alley echoed off the walls like pistol shots. One on each side of the central sewage channel they dodged around broken chairs and abandoned carts. A wizened old man covered in white sores and wearing only a grubby dhoti slept on a lopsided charpoy, the only sign of life in the shuttered, bolted and deserted slum.

Keeping the sun always ahead of them and the noise of the angry crowd behind them, they ran until the darkness of the alleyways ended in the bright glare of noon at Victoria Road.

They paused to catch their breath, hearing the cries and screams of the gathering mob swell with each passing second. The bearer took his young charge by the hand and started across the wide road but they had scarcely reached halfway when a panic-stricken human tidal wave fleeing from the violence engulfed them. Before they could be swept off their feet, Gulameer took Sikander in his arms and fought his way through the surging crowd. They found temporary safety crouching behind the fountain and statue of the young queen that dominated the centre of the intersection.

The howling flood of humanity streamed past them. A few feet away, a young woman with a baby in her arms staggered. The infant pitched from her arms when the woman fell and for a second Sikander lost sight of them. He heard a scream. Then the frenzied runners following the woman trampled her, slipping and stumbling in the fresh blood left by her and her baby. Unable to avert his eyes, Sikander stared open-mouthed at the ragged, bloody bundles lying motionless on the earth and grasped the significance of the first violent deaths he had witnessed.

At that moment, all of Sikander's worldly insouciance evaporated. He covered his eyes with his shaking hands. His freckled face turned ashen. With trembling knees, he sank to the ground, doubled over, and retched.

When the slowest and last of the refugees passed the fountain, Gulameer took Sikander by the hand. "Come, Chota Sahib," he said. "We go this way." Sikander allowed himself to be pulled along blindly on rubbery legs. He heard Gulameer say, "We go to the Christian church, Chota Sahib. We will be safe there."

Sikander placed his faith and all the trust of his eight years in his mother's bearer. He tightened his grip on the bearer's hand, certain that Gulameer would lead them to safety. They ran across the road and through the dusty gardens of the Anglican cathedral. When they reached the top of the steps at the west entrance, they stopped, hearts pounding, doubled over and sucking in lungfuls of air.

Gulameer straightened and grasped the wrought-iron handle of the wooden door. When the door failed to budge, he put his shoulder to it again and again in a desperate attempt to force it open. He turned back as the first of a seething mass of armed men headed directly for the church. With nowhere to run and nowhere to hide, Sikander knew they were trapped between the building and hundreds of men crazed with blood lust and bent on killing.

Statue-still, Gulameer faced the mob, waiting until the lead runners neared to within a hundred feet of the steps. Only then did he raise his right hand high above his head, and bellow in Bengali, "Parade . . . Halt!"

Confronted only by the bearer and the small boy standing properly at attention as if he too were on parade, the runners at the front slowed and stopped at the foot of the steps. A menacing roar from their throats swelled to a frenzied howl before dying away.

In the calm that followed, Gulameer drew himself up to his full height. In his immaculate grey military-style household tunic and baggy trousers, puttees and bright red Regimental cockade exactly centred on his spotless turban, he looked every inch the regimental sergeant major. He fixed his attention on a man in the front rank of the armed rabble, a man in a dirty, ragged shirt spotted with bright arterial blood who clutched a glistening, red-streaked sword in his hand. This was a man, Sikander understood instinctively, who had recently killed.

"I am Gulameer Abdul Ali Khan," the bearer shouted in Bengali. "I was a subadar major in the Fourth Bengal Lancers, a loyal Muslim Regiment. I served Bengal for over twenty years. I fear no army. I fear no man. I fear only almighty Allah."

Gulameer paused for a moment, staring into the eyes of the blood-spattered man in the front rank. "I am not an idolatrous cow-worshiper. I am an unworthy servant of Allah. If I die at your hands today, so be it. I am a Hajj. My entry to paradise is assured. My life counts for little. The English

Chota Sahib has done you no wrong. If Allah should judge that you acted wrongly you will receive the punishment of his almighty wrath for all eternity. I am less than a grain of sand in Allah's great universe, and the Chota Sahib is too young to be held accountable for his father's sins."

Sikander stood motionless at his bearer's side, old enough to understand the danger the angry men presented and old enough to fear them.

"If your anger is at the East India Company," Gulameer said in a quieter voice, "that I understand. I too have suffered indignities and beatings at their hands. There is no love in my heart for their officials, for they have only contempt for us and our beliefs." He raised his voice to a shout. "They are pig-eating foreigners. They deserve to spend eternity in the hell-fires of damnation with the great diseased whore of Satan."

Gulameer set his face in an expressionless mask and with Sikander boy watching at his side waited in silence as the sword of their fate hung by the thinnest of threads above their heads. The decision whether they lived or died lay in the hands of the blood-spattered, wild-eyed man in front of them.

The silence stretched until the man in the front rank slowly raised his bloody sword above his head. He turned fully to face the men behind him. A throaty roar rose to greet him, calling for death. The man shook his head and the noise abated.

"The subadar major speaks the truth," he shouted. "Our fight is with the British, and the East India Company, not with one of our own. Almighty Allah commands that we will let the subadar major and the boy live." He waved his sword. "We will let them live."

The man lowered his sword and turned to face Gulameer. A murmur of grudging approval rose and swelled over the man's back. Only the small boy beside his mother's bearer standing parade ground-rigid heard the subadar major exhale.

"By your good grace, we go now, the Chota Sahib and me," Gulameer said quietly to the bloody man in the front rank. "But the army will soon be here with their rifles. If you do not return to your homes immediately, they will hunt you down. They will kill you with the same mercy as they show a pi-dog."

He waited a moment for his words to hit home. "Your wives will be widows before sunset, and your sons fatherless. They will desecrate your bodies and throw Hindu and Muslim together into the same lime pit with pigs and dogs. That is their way of heaping scorn and insult upon our heads."

Gulameer took Sikander by the hand and descended the cathedral steps. The crowd parted to let them through, and without a backward glance they set off in the direction of Sikander's home.

"Gulameer?" Sikander asked after they had left the church grounds and crossed the main road.

"Yes, Chota Sahib?"

"Were you really a subadar major?"

"No. I was only a subadar, a sergeant, but if they knew that they would not have listened to me. Without a doubt, they would consider me of no account, a lover of the English and the East India Company. But a subadar major is an important man in the army, a man worthy of respect."

"You are very brave, Gulameer."

They walked on in silence until they came to the gates of Sikander's house.

"Gulameer," he said while they waited for the gatekeeper to unlock the wrought iron gates for them. "I have one other question."

Gulameer looked down at the young boy. "And what is your question, Chota Sahib?"

"What's a whore?"

26.   THE BOX

By Raymond Holmes

My young eyes didn't see our poverty and hardship then, but later on Mama told us about how bad things were and why we left Holland. It's hard to believe my family came here over so long ago. A black and white photograph is one of the few keepsakes I have from when we left the Netherlands in 1955.

The years of conflict and occupation during the Second World War had taken their toll on the Dutch people. Hunger, brutality, sickness and economic stagnation had caused widespread suffering. After the war ended, jobs were scarce and there seemed little opportunity for families of modest means. My parents wanted a better life for themselves and their three children.

Why not immigrate to another country? Other Dutch people had gone to the America's and elsewhere. Those countries were large, rich and young—not old, tired, and class-structured like Europe. Letters sent back by relatives and former neighbours were filled with stories of prosperity: plenty of work, abundant food and beautiful wide-open spaces. A family had the opportunity to own a home or farm—even a motor vehicle.

It must have been a difficult decision for my parents, a couple almost forty years of age at the time with three young children. They had never ventured far from the small town of their birth near the German border, and the journey would be long.

Papa travelled by train to the foreign consulates in Arnhem and applied to Australia, South Africa, New Zealand, the United States, and Canada.

The first four countries rejected us. My younger sister Martina had a medical condition that would require treatment to correct. They decided she'd be a burden to their societies. It looked like that new life for our family wouldn't happen. One day a letter came from the Canadian Consulate accepting us. We were already indebted to that wonderful country for liberating us from the Germans and now they were opening their door to us.

The photograph taken before our departure makes those sixty-five year-old memories flood in. How dour and apprehensive we all look standing in our front yard. Life would change forever, and even as children, we sensed it. Our parents spoke little English. The challenges they faced must have seemed like mountains they would have to cross.

My mind transforms the monotone hue of the old photograph into the colours of that day so long ago. My sister and I were dressed in the same robin's egg blue dresses. We were two years apart in age, but Mama thought our identical outfits would look nice in that last photograph in front of our old home. At least we didn't look like our older brother Willem. He wore a grey suit with knickers that flared out at his thighs and formed into buttoned cuffs at the knee. I don't think he's ever been as stylishly attired as he was that day. We were excited, but sorrowful as well, having to leave the only home we'd ever known, a large extended family, virtually all of our possessions and everything familiar. Sad farewells were bid to uncles, aunts, cousins, and friends we might never see again. Our toys were given away.

Papa was a carpenter by trade and built a wooden box to hold our worldly goods for the journey. We could only take a few possessions due to the high cost of shipment to Canada. Inside were three thin, rolled-up mattresses, Papa's tools, Mama's few pieces of cherished Delft china, and a small cabinet to hold them. We children were allowed only a small suitcase each—no toys or books. That luggage would hold clothing and toiletry items for a journey of more than ten days. Papa bought each of us girls a pair of red leather boots. He said we'd need those in Canada.

"Anna—go next door and bring me back an egg. Don't break it," he said to me.

I wondered why he was taking a raw egg to Canada.

Papa cracked the shell, separated the yolk out, and used the egg white as an adhesive to affix the paper address label to the side of the box. Late at night, I crept downstairs and stared at that crate sitting on the kitchen floor illuminated by moonlight shining through the front window. It seemed to say, "Your family's life is in here." The wooden box seemed small, considering it contained the worldly possessions of five people.

The next morning a grey van arrived at the house and we loaded the wooden box, our suitcases, and ourselves into the vehicle. Perhaps the trip wouldn't be that long if we were driving there, I reasoned. I fell asleep in the back seat dreaming of the beautiful house we would have in Canada with the mountains in the background. It would be just like the pictures Uncle Gustav had shown us in a book several days earlier. My mind imagined the sound of clear, rushing water and wind blowing through the trees.

Someone shook me. "Wake up. We're here," Mama said.

I rubbed my eyes and squinted into the bright sunlight. A large boat rested beside a long pier. I looked up at the mammoth vessel, its tethering ropes thicker than my leg.

"What does that word on the side of the boat say?" I asked Mama.

"It says 'Waterman.' That's the name of the boat. We'll sail on it to our new home in Canada."

A boat with water in its name—appropriate. They unloaded our box, put it onto a cart and took it away. We could see a huge derrick lifting piles of other boxes onto the ship. Papa hurried us toward the long gangway leading up onto the deck. I kept looking back, worried that our box wouldn't be loaded aboard.

We followed the line of passengers walking up the ramp, holding onto our suitcases with one hand and the rope railing with the other. Other families like ours were embarking on this great adventure: mothers and fathers leading young children and holding small babies in their arms. The walk up to the deck of the ship must have been painful for Mama. Later on, we found out she'd fallen from her bicycle the day before and broke her ankle.

On board, quivering with exhilaration, I peered through the deck railing at the bustling port of Rotterdam, much of it still in ruins from the terrible bombing during the war. The loudness of the ship's horn blast startled me. The vessel cast off its moorings and slipped leisurely through the harbour towards the open water. Sadness crawled into me as I watched the land shrink, and finally disappear. We were now somewhere between two worlds, not belonging to either one.

More excitement came in the following days, but not the kind I wanted. We were berthed in steerage on an old, converted troop ship. Sea sickness was my companion for ten long, agonizing days due to the rocking, rolling, rising and falling North Atlantic Ocean. I was hungry but repulsed by the food. It wasn't the good, Dutch home cooking we were accustomed to. If only I had some of Mama's homemade soup to eat—that might stay in my stomach. Papa had the same malady and was bed-ridden. I stared at my pale, sickly face in the mirror. If we had to endure this much suffering to reach Canada, I wanted no part of it. I cried and begged to go back home.

Eventually my tears stopped and fear subsided. I became resigned to dying. Death would free me from misery. My eyes would never see Canada, the beautiful land.

One afternoon, through the haze of a restless nap, came the sound of animated voices and moving feet. I felt a soft bump as the side of the ship nudged an object.

"Get up," Mama said. "The ship has docked in Canada."

We hugged and danced in circles. Tears flowed.

"Be happy, children. It's a new life for us," Mama said as we stood on deck watching the activity on shore.

All around us people were cheering and clapping their hands. Someone said this was a city called Halifax in the province called Nova Scotia.

Now we could leave this uncomfortable, floating home. Whatever the future held, it couldn't be any worse than this journey had been.

Mama pointed at a building. "See that sign? We're at Pier 21," she said, as they herded us down the gangway and into a room in a large building.

The sensation of walking on land again and not feeling the movement of the boat was strange. I've had an aversion to boats ever since and never did learn how to swim.

My brother Willem's face bore a sour look. "I hope they don't let us in," he said, as we inched forward in the long, slow line of fellow immigrants. Thirteen years old and homesick for his friends, he hoped we would be sent back to Holland. Children wailed, and parents stretched their necks sideways to see why things were taking so long.

Squeak-thump. Squeak-thump. The sound of stamps pounding on paper echoed off the walls.

"What a wonderful job to have," Papa said. "Being paid just to stamp people's documents. Governments are the same all over the world."

The agent looked us over.

"You're a farmer, Mister Van Zandt?"

"Yes," Papa said.

Mama gave Papa a surprised look but knew better than to say anything.

"Your sponsor is Mister John Blackstone in Ontario?"

"Yes. We go to him in Alliston town."

Another man in a white coat approached.

"Stick out your tongues. Any sickness or fever with your family?"

"No," Mama and Papa replied in unison.

"Papa and I threw up on the boat," I said.

Mama grabbed my arm and shook me. "Be quiet Anna." She put her hand over my mouth. "It was only the sea sickness, sir."

The man smiled at me and passed Papa a piece of paper. "Welcome to Canada."

Papa looked at the document, at the man, then Mama. That was it?

We wouldn't be going back to Holland like Willem wanted. I was happy. The last thing I wanted to do was to get back on that boat.

After we passed through immigration, Mama took me and Martina into a secluded corner. "Don't either one of you say another word until we're on the train. If you're bad they'll send us back," she said.

Mama's broken foot hurt her a lot so she went to the Red Cross first aid station. After a huddled discussion, they took her away.

Martina and I cried. "Mama—Mama. Don't leave us." Where were they taking her? Would we ever see her again?

A lady in a blue dress with a funny cap on her head offered us brown, fizzy liquid to drink. We stopped crying. It was sweet and the bubbles tickling my nose made me sneeze.

She pointed at the cup and said, "Coca Cola. Good—yes?"

The English language was strange and what they drank in Canada even stranger.

It seemed like a long time, but Mama finally returned, hobbling with her foot encased in a white boot. We ran into her arms and hugged her so hard she almost fell down. We lined up to board the train. I'll never forget the sight of it. Stunning—like a sleek, green and black snake curling away into the distance, glistening in the sunshine; so long we couldn't see the end of it. A plume of smoke curled up from the locomotive.

"We're still a long way from our home in Ontario province," Mama said.

A man in a uniform blew on a whistle. "All aboard," he said.

Our small legs were too short to negotiate the first step so Papa lifted Martina and I into the coach. My very first train ride.

"Sit down and be quiet," Mama said.

Soon the car jerked. "We're moving. We're moving," I yelled.

"I told you to be quiet, Anna. Don't make me have to tell you again," Mama said.

The train gathered speed and the April maritime landscape passed by in a green ribbon interrupted by the dark dashes of telephone poles. Houses, farms, lakes and small communities with strange names flashed by. The land wasn't flat and featureless like Holland. The rolling hills seemed like mountains and we passed through thick forests with giant trees that seemed to go on forever. Everything was new and different. My head burst with questions about our new home, my school in Canada, learning a new language and meeting new friends. It was a great adventure and my future a series of blank pages ready to draw on.

"Why did the immigration agent say you were a farmer," Mama finally asked Papa. "You're a carpenter."

Papa could build anything from wood. There were many farms in The Netherlands, but we weren't farmers.

"When we applied to Canada, they asked my occupation. I'm a carpenter, I told them. 'We don't need carpenters', they replied. We need farmers."

"Then why did they accept us?" Mama said.

"I said carpentry was my second job, farming the first."

Mama's face whitened like something had sucked all the blood out of her head. "God help us. We know nothing about farming. Why didn't you tell me?"

Papa didn't answer. The stunned expression on Mama's face turned to silent anger. Tears formed at the corners of her eyes. She didn't say anything for a long time after.

Monotonous hours of watching the world outside the train, interspersed with broken sleep rubbed the novelty off the journey. Martina got motion sick, but I was fine. The train stopped once, but we didn't get off.

Eventually we arrived at Union Station in Toronto; so many trains sitting side by side on numerous tracks.

After wandering through stone corridors and climbing many stairs, we reached the large, open area of the station concourse, the most beautiful building I had ever seen. The high arches, expansive space and tall, classical columns reminded me of a fairy-tale castle. Mama and Papa scanned the swirling tide of humanity all around us, searching for the man who would meet us and be our sponsor—the farmer from Alliston, Ontario. We had memorized the name of that place, saying it over and over. Alliston—Alliston—as if it was a precious object.

We were alone in a large, strange city, had no accommodation, and knew no one.

Mama put her hands around Martina and my shoulders, drawing us close. "What if he's not here?" she asked Papa, her voice trembling and face creased with worry.

He didn't answer and moved his head side to side surveying the faces passing by.

"There!" Papa said, extending his hand and pointing. We saw a man holding a cardboard sign with our name hand-written on it in black lettering.

"Thank God," Mama cried. She grabbed our hands and pulled us toward him.

"You are Mr. Blackstone?" Papa said to the man.

"Yes, and you are the Van Zandt family, I presume. Welcome to Canada."

Papa shook his hand so vigorously Mr. Blackstone's head bobbed up and down and his hat slipped back. "That is us. Thank you sir."

Mama smiled for the first time since Papa announced on the train that they would be doing farm work. You could see the tide of relief rise on her face and the tension release from her small body. I was glad this long, difficult journey was over and wondered what my room would be like in our new house.

"I'm hungry," Martina said.

Mama shushed her. The man looked down and smiled.

Mister Blackstone towered over me, staring down with cold, bright blue eyes. He wore faded grey overalls with a red plaid shirt and a brown, wide brimmed hat soiled with rings of dried perspiration. He picked up two of our suitcases and led us to his old pick-up truck.

Our box, which I had forgotten about, rested on the bed of the truck with the label still affixed to it. Mister Blackstone, Mama and Papa got into the front seat. Martina sat on Papa's lap. Willem and I huddled in the open back of the pick-up truck beside the wooden box and luggage.

After a long, bumpy drive sitting on the corrugated metal bed of the truck, shivering in the chilly, April Ontario air, we arrived at our new home. It was hard to say which was more uncomfortable, my sore backside or empty stomach.

The house, a one-and-a half storey dwelling on a potato farm in Alliston, Ontario, wasn't as beautiful as I had imagined. Where were the ice-capped mountains and the clear, rushing river shown in the pictures? Mister Blackstone gave us some sandwiches made with white bread and funny tasting orange liquid to drink. I lifted the slices of bread apart to look at the thin layer in between.

"Bologna," he said. The bread wasn't good and dark like that in Holland. Did people in Canada eat like this?

In the morning, white plumes of my breath drifted in the air inside the house and my teeth chattered. The ice-cold, cracked, red, yellow and brown linoleum floor made my ankles ache. No wood for the stove. If it would just warm up things might not be so bad. It wasn't like our beautiful house in The Netherlands that Mama kept so clean.

"All I need is some soap and water. It'll be just like back home," she said.

Holland wasn't home anymore. In this new place there was a rough dirt road, a few trees, some grass and fields of dark, frost covered, cultivated earth stretching as far as you could see. How did they make the furrows so straight?

Papa opened the wooden box and took out our few possessions. Mama's small cabinet and Delft-blue china made it seem more like home. Papa's ingenuity amazed me. He built the box so that when he took it apart, the pieces could be assembled into a kitchen table and benches with no wood left over.

Mr. Blackstone conscripted Mama, Papa and Willem to work on the farm. Martina and I sat at the edge of the fields amusing ourselves by creating stories, singing songs and twisting long blades of grass together into shapes we fantasized were companions. I thought of our real dolls given away in Holland now cradled in the arms of other children. Sometimes we were naughty and ate the lunches that Mama had prepared for the whole family. She scolded us for being thoughtless and selfish. That memory still makes me feel ashamed.

Life in our first Canadian home was hard. The conditions were little more than slavery. Mister Blackstone turned out to be a hard, humourless, miserly taskmaster, not the benefactor we had imagined. The work was backbreaking in blistering heat, rain and cold for little pay. If Papa questioned or objected to something, he was told how lucky we were to have a sponsor and if we didn't co-operate he could send us back.

I didn't understand why Papa became so angry and cross with us all the time. Later on, I realized that as head of the family, he felt responsible for bringing us to Canada and was worried about our future. There was no one else to bear the brunt of his frustration.

We barely had enough to eat. I was never hungry in Holland.

"I could write a book on one hundred ways to cook potatoes, onions and carrots," Mama said years later. Much of the time that's all we had. Our clothing was inadequate. Nobody told us how cold Canada would be for several months of the year. I crawled up the steep, slippery hill to go to school in the winter and understood why Papa wanted us to have the red boots. If only they'd been warmer. So much snow. It looked like a thick layer of whipped cream covered the land—fun to play in if you were dressed warm enough. Someone said that people in the distant Canadian northland called Eskimos lived in snow houses. I didn't believe that.

With no farm work during the winter season, Papa took a job in town building coffins so we could survive. Someone gave him an old bicycle, so he didn't have to walk.

"It's good to work with wood again, even if the end product is for dead people," he said. When he arrived home at night, his clothes bore the fragrant aromas of oak, pine and cedar. I helped pick off the wood shavings stuck to his clothes. Papa was happy until one afternoon in January, 1956.

He came home trembling with a migraine headache. It was the first time I'd seen him cry. In town he'd heard horrific, devastating news. An immigrant man who lived in our house before us had committed suicide there.

Their dreams of a new life in Canada having become a hideous nightmare, that man's widow and children returned to their homeland. We had no money to go back to Holland. Papa became obsessed with wondering how and where in the house the man had ended his life. Were they sleeping or standing on the very spot? Was that stain on the pine floor from a pool of blood? Did he hang himself from that rafter with the mark on it?

Papa couldn't escape the feeling that he'd brought his family here to perish and would be making coffins for all of us. Life in that house became unbearable for him.

One night shortly after, Martina and I awoke to the sound of hammering. Creeping downstairs I saw that Papa had dismantled the kitchen table and benches and was rebuilding the box.

Excited, I hurried back upstairs, jumped into bed beside my sister and pulled the covers up over our heads. "We're going back to Holland," I whispered to her.

We fell asleep happy, dreaming of the family and friends we would see again after all those long months. Perhaps we could get our toys back.

The agreement our family made obliged us to stay on that farm for one year, but Mama wrote to a distant cousin in Burlington, Ontario describing our plight and begging him to help us get away.

Three nights later, we heard tapping on our door. Mama greeted her cousin as if he was our saviour, the Lord Jesus himself.

"You children must be very quiet," she said several times in a desperate, frightened whisper.

We, the wooden box, and our other possessions were quietly loaded into the cousin's van. He released the hand brake and the vehicle coasted down the hill from the house with its lights off. When at the road, he started the motor and we escaped into the dark night. Mama kept looking back over her shoulder while grasping our hands so tightly they hurt.

"It's all right children," she said over and over again.

After driving for forty minutes in complete silence Martina said in a small voice, "Can we talk now?"

We didn't return to the Netherlands. Mama's cousin helped us find a place to live and Papa found work as a carpenter. When we could afford a store-bought table and chairs, Papa used the wood from the box to make a bench. My sister Martina has it in her home now. I sit on it whenever we visit her and can almost feel the memories seeping out from that worn, burnished wood. It seems to say, "I'm a part of your family. You couldn't have done it without me."

Life in Canada improved. Mama and Papa worked hard, saved their money and purchased a home. We became citizens, received educations and enjoyed successful careers.

What would it have been like if we'd stayed in Europe? Life's like that—a choice of paths arriving at different destinations. That "what if" crosses my mind from time to time. I'm proud of my accomplishments here in Canada, but also of my Dutch heritage.

I think of Mama and Papa often and marvel at their courage in leaving all they had, travelling across the ocean and struggling to make a better life. They rest in Canadian soil, their adopted country, far from Holland. Mama's little china cabinet looks out of place in my dining room, but I'll never part with it. The old, wind-up alarm clock that announced the start of their working days for so many years is a knick-knack on my shelf now.

I still worry about that potato farm in Alliston. Our contract still has four months to run. My husband says I'd better be good to him or he'll report me.

ABOUT THE AUTHORS

CHERRY NARULA

Born in India, Cherry pursued studies in English and French literature, followed by an airline career. She moved to Brampton, Canada, 25 years ago. She published her first book in December 2020, titled *Nona and Daniel – Taming the Monkey*, which is dedicated to all grandparents. Cherry believes that one thing constant in life is 'learning', and life can be continuously enriched, without a single dull moment, by taking a flight to read and learn.

KEN PUDDICOMBE

Ken Puddicombe is a retired CPA. *Racing With The Rain*, his first novel was released in 2012. His second novel *Junta* was published in 2014. His collection of short stories *Down Independence Boulevard* was released in 2017. His first book of poems *Unfathomable and Other Poems* was released in 2020. All his books were published by www.middleroadpublishers.ca. His website: http://www.kenpuddicombe.ca.

LYNDA BRUNELLE

Lynda Brunelle has been writing since she was twelve years old. She loves everything from historical fiction, romance and cozy mystery. When she's not reading or writing, she can be found flying the friendly skies as a flight attendant. She lives in Brampton with her husband and four year old daughter and one year old son and two Cavalier King Charles Spaniels- Sawyer and Murphy.

MARK BLAIR

MARK BLAIR won praise and one national award for writing and debating in high school. He was founder and editor of his department's student newsletter at university, instrumental in influencing policy decisions affecting the program and student life. His education and career is in Computer Science applied in the fields of education, health, insurance and finance. He writes for pleasure. Now an active member of the Peel writing community, he leads the Brampton Library Memoirs Writing Group and serves as Editor of the Mississauga Writers Group's quarterly Write ON! with responsibility for curating and editing content, and designing and publishing for web and print.

MICHAEL JOLL

Michael Joll has called Brampton home since 1975. Born and raised mostly in England, with lengthy childhood stays in India and Pakistan, he and his wife immigrated to Canada in 1973. He has authored and had three plays performed on Canadian Public Radio. In addition he has dozens of short stories to his credit, many of them award winners. Several of his stories have appeared in magazines and anthologies. His first collection, *Perfect Execution and Other Stories* was published in 2017. A second series of stories, *Persons of Interest*, appeared in 2019. His first novel, *A Time To Love and a Time To Die*, was published by MiddleRoadPublishers in 2020. He currently serves as President of the Brampton Writers Guild.

RAYMOND HOLMES

Raymond Holmes was born and raised in Toronto and lives in Brampton, Ontario. Following careers in Industry he started writing upon retirement in spite of being seriously challenged by English grammar. His plays *Boris and Herman, The Pooman* and *The Lonely Vigil Of Emily Baxter* were performed at the South Simcoe Theatre in Cookstown, Ontario. The last play listed went on to greater success, winning third prize plus a reading in the 2013 Ottawa Little Theatre playwriting contest. Raymond has authored two books: *Witnesses And Other Short Stories* published by MiddleRoad Publishers in

2019, and *A Barber's Son – Recollections of Growing Up In 1950's Toronto*, published by Eleventh Street Press. He has had work published in *The Northern Appeal*, a bi-annual Simcoe County literary journal, and *Unleashed Ink II*, an anthology of short stories and poetry published by the Barrie Writers Club.

RENA FLANNIGAN

Rena is now in the fourth level of discovering her talents and encourages you to reach out and find yours. From a small town in Scotland to Canada, which was a place she only knew from movies, she set off, almost broke, to a new life in 1952. Destiny took her through various occupations, all of which she enjoyed for many years before she finally discovered she could be a writer. As a tailoress and fur finisher, a teacher of fashion, tour manager, her favourite job where she could travel keeping up with her fantasies of other destinations. Rena invites you to share them, exploring some of her journey, reading her stories and poems.

RACING WITH THE RAIN

By Ken Puddicombe

"Ken Puddicombe's brilliant novel…an historic political conflict in Guyana, during the Cold War and the cold cynicism and tragic irony of a state sacrificed to super-power hegemony." -Frank Birbalsingh, author of *Novels and The Nation: Essays in Canadian*

JUNTA

By Ken Puddicombe

"A gripping story (of) an imperfect democracy…the tension…builds increasingly from page to page."—Rico Downer, author of *There Once Was a Little England*

DOWN INDEPENDENCE BOULEVARD AND OTHER STORIES

by Ken Puddicombe

"A brilliant collection of stories telling the tales of people forced to leave their homes…craving the past, escaping from racial conflicts and dictatorship…"—Judith Kopacsi Gelberger, author of *Heroes Don't Cry*.

PERFECT EXECUTION

by Michael Joll.

"Michael Joll is a master of surprise endings, but they never seem forced. He always stays true to his characters and their worlds." —Nancy Kay Clark, author and editor, *CommuterLit.com*

PERSONS OF INTEREST

By Michael Joll

"Exotic and intriguing! Joll brilliantly captures the reader's interest with vivid imagery and a relentless sleuth." —Phyllis Humby, short story writer, poet and novelist.

WITNESSES AND

OTHER STORIES

By Raymond Holmes

"Whether comedic or tragic, plunge his readers into vivid slightly askew worlds, where violins hold memories, suitcases vanish, ghosts abound and death waits behind every door."—Nancy Kay Clark, author of *The Prince of Sudland: Escape from the Palace*.

ATTITUDE

By Dave Moores

Fresh, gritty and laced with dry humour, Attitude is a fast-paced story readers of all ages won't want to put down. It's dead of winter and an outbreak of weird stuff, random acts of vandalism are unsettling the citizens of Southmead.

POEMS FOR MARY

By Ian Mc Donald

"The garden which my wife has created, it is as much a work of art as a painting by a master spirit or a piece of perfect music by a composer."—Ian Mc Donald

UNFATHOMABLE AND OTHER POEMS

by Ken Puddicombe

These poems cover a variety of themes, all connected to a childhood growing up in British Guiana, the rise of nationalism and the pre- and post-independence eras.

I WENT TO THE END OF THE RAINBOW

by Pramita Chakraborty

A beautifully illustrated, captivating tale about a young child who can't sleep and embarks on a adventure through the colours of the rainbow.

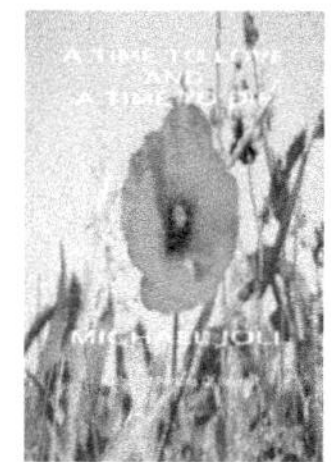

A TIME TO LOVE AN A TIME TO DIE

By Michael Joll

Finely drawn characters. Visually dramatic, tense and emotionally satisfying, this is one of the finest novels of the Great War. In this poignant story, the writing stands in stark contrast with the unvarnished brutality of trench warfare.